SOFTBALL
FOR WEEKEND WARRIORS

SOFTBALL
FOR WEEKEND WARRIORS

A GUIDE TO EVERYTHING FROM HOMERS TO
HAPPY HOURS TO PULLED HAMSTRINGS

RANDY HOWE

THE LYONS PRESS
Guilford, Connecticut
An imprint of The Globe Pequot Press

Disclaimer

The names of teams, sponsors, leagues, and mixed drinks in this book are not fictitious. The people and stories, neither. Exaggerated, maybe. Altered in my favor, perhaps. But definitely not nonfiction. Definitely not . . .

Copyright © 2005 by Randy Howe

Photographs copyright ©2005 by Randy Howe

ALL RIGHTS RESERVED. No part of this book may be reproduced or transmitted in any form by any means, electronic or mechanical, including photocopying and recording, or by any information storage and retrieval system, except as may be expressly permitted in writing from the publisher. Requests for permission should be addressed to The Lyons Press, Attn: Rights and Permissions Department, P.O. Box 480, Guilford, CT 06437.

The Lyons Press is an imprint of The Globe Pequot Press.

10 9 8 7 6 5 4 3 2 1

Printed in the United States of America

Designed by Maggie Peterson

Library of Congress Cataloging-in-Publication Data.
    Howe, Randy.
        Softball for weekend warriors : a guide to everything from pulled
        hamstrings to homers to happy hours / Randy Howe.
            p. cm.
        Includes bibliographical references.
        ISBN 1-59228-611-9 (trade paper)
        1. Softball. I. Title.
    GV881.H69 2005
    796.357'8—dc22
                                2005003114

To all the Payne Environmentalists.

Acknowledgments

A debt of gratitude to...
Ann, for being such a good sport.
Willie, for lending me the latest in AV technology.
Matt, Joe, Jon, and Tucker,
for being such super supermodels!
Bill Plummer III, for lending this book some legitimacy.
And finally Alicia, for not only tolerating my athletic
infatuations but encouraging them.

Prelude

It has long been my dream to dig in, my right foot burrowing into the back of the batter's box while with my left foot I do the twist; to spit with confidence while my eyes take in the positioning of the outfielders; to say something that will prickle the catcher but make the umpire smile; to know that my teammates have faith; to feel, with absolute certainty, that their faith will be rewarded.

It has long been my dream to say screw taking the first pitch; to hitch ever so slightly as the ball leaves like lightning the fingertips of the pitcher, bound for a destiny not yet known; to read the seams of a hanging slider and to watch as the baseball rockets off of the sweet spot of my Louisville Slugger, floating through the night sky, high above them all like a second moon. High enough to glide beyond the center fielder's reach before landing in the bleachers for a game-winning home run. To slow down as I round first and then to nod with appreciation as the shortstop says, "Nice shot."

In reality, there is no one-liner, no hanging slider, no baseball, no wooden bat, no gracious shortstop. There isn't any fence-clearing tater, either. Not even close.

What there is . . . is reality.

And the reality is that I use a $300, 34-ounce, double-walled graphite bat named after some long-dead conquistador to miss-hit a weak blooper into shallow left. And just when you think it could get no worse, while rounding first I realize that I'm too slow to turn this gift of a single into a double. Too far to go back and not far enough to make a go of it, I stop in my tracks. Gone is the dream. I fart dust.

Yes, reality has turned nightmarish because I'm now caught between first and second in the classic pickle. I feel like the guy Bugs Bunny beats to a pulp in the cartoon, Bugs rounding the bases in a conga line and the other guy hapless and helpless—what was his name? Ah yes, The Crusher!—except I'm the one who's about to get crushed. Even worse, embarrassed. Explicit hazing awaits as does certain defeat.

But what's this? Bad is starting to look good as the infielders who chase me back and forth, back and forth, seem to have forgotten about the runner on third. I am just quick enough to avoid their tags. The Force is with me as I anticipate the exact moment to put on the brakes and head back in the other direction. This distraction—three or four chubby guys in red chasing one chubby guy in blue pinstripes—lasts long enough for my man on third to jet home with the winning run. The throw arrives late, I suck in some much-needed oxygen, and the three softball widows who've come out to give their support gladly flee for home. Not us, though. Not we conquistadors of the Madison "B" League. No, we hug, high-five, and hyperventilate around home plate before stumbling off of the field towards the bar. Payne wins! Payne wins!! Payne wins!!!

This is slow-pitch softball at its finest.

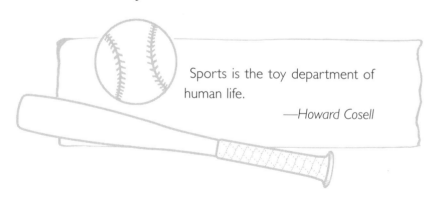

Sports is the toy department of human life.

—Howard Cosell

Table of Contents

Introduction: Weekend Warriors Are We xiii

1. From Slow-Pitch to Sixteen-Inch:
   Variations of the Game 1

2. Weekend Warrior Hall of Fame: Eddie Feigner 19

3. When You Just Don't Have the Skills
   to Pay the Bills 21

4. Weekend Warrior Hall of Fame: Ty Stofflet 41

5. "But honey, look . . . I'm losin' weight!" 43

6. Gluteus Maximus and Other Muscles
   Just Waiting to Be Pulled 51

7. Weekend Warrior Hall of Fame: Bill Leete 67

8. Earning a Call 69

9. Weekend Warrior Hall of Fame: Bill Plummer III . . . 77

10. Talking the Talk (Even If You Can't Quite
    Walk the Walk) 79

11. Weekend Warrior Hall of Fame:
    Mr. Rotisserie Baseball . . . Daniel Okrent 87

12. You Got Gear 89

13. Weekend Warrior Hall of Fame:
    The Hooters Championship Series 99

14. Why Softball is Actually Better Than Baseball 101

15. You've Got Game Now,
    But No Idea Where to Play It 105

16. Charity Begins at Home (Plate) 111

17. A Return to Couchdom 115

Closing: You're Never Too Old
to Break Up a Double Play 121

Bibliography 125

From the Webster's Old School Dictionary

game¹ (gām) noun **1** any form of play or way of playing; amusement; recreation; sport; frolic **2** any specific contest, engagement, self-injurious behavior involving a score, other players, beer, trash talk, scabs, sweat, physical feats of mind-over-matter, stakes (meaning risk, not wood, metal, or plastic, although those are sometimes involved, as well) **3** a way or quality of playing in competition **4** any test of skill, courage, or endurance **5** wild animals that are hunted and killed and displayed over the mantel after being mercy-ruled [1]

game² (gām) adjective **1** to be lame or injured

---

[1] *The flesh is often consumed at barbecues, too. Yummy!*

Introduction:
Weekend Warriors Are We

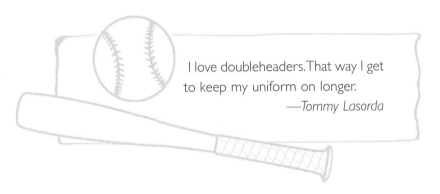

I love doubleheaders. That way I get
to keep my uniform on longer.
—*Tommy Lasorda*

To be a weekend warrior is to be a player. It is to love sports and, at times, to do foolish things while playing sports. It is to do foolish things just to get away for a couple of hours to play sports. That being said, the term "weekend warrior" really has no set definition. As evidence of this, being a weekend warrior has very little to do with Saturday and Sunday. We weekend warriors seek games not two days a week but seven. Most of us mortgage totin', minivan drivin', in-law entertainin', ass kissin', paint the kitchen, quit your bitchin', seven-year itchin' (just for the sake of the rhyme, hon) midlife crisis candidates once sought greater things than this. The stuff of legend . . .

When April rolls around, I still dust off the ol' cleats and rub shaving cream into my glove. I do butterfly stretches to preserve my groin; I pull the heating pad out of the closet and test its powers of rejuvenation; I make sure there are ample ice packs in the freezer, all in anticipation of the upcoming season. No, not a season that will build up to Joe Buck and Tim McCarver on a cool October night, the Goodyear blimp high overhead and 56,000 in attendance, but a season of softball by the shore. Madison Beach and Rec "B" League slow-pitch softball, to be exact. And I couldn't be happier about it.

Of course we all grow up wanting to be the next legend. We dream of ending a playoff game with the long ball, with one mighty swing of Wonder Boy à la Robert Redford and Kirk Gibson and Joe Carter. We want to hurl lightning like Roger Clemens and Randy Johnson and The Rookie. We want to be fast like Rickey Henderson and smooth like Derek Jeter (on the field and off!). But somewhere along the way, reality settled in, didn't it? In all likelihood, we lucked into a winning team in Little League and then life started its downhill descent. We made the freshman team by the skin of our teeth, blackmailed the coach for a spot on the JV, but then turned to the golf team after failing to make the varsity. Perhaps the end came when we tore an ACL or maybe it was that we were forced to graduate. Maybe, if we were decent enough, that graduation was college rather than high school and maybe we were still playing at the time. Even if this was the case, the writing was still on the wall. Leagues became as hard to find as the time to play. For some, the finale came with the sacrificial joy of parenthood. For others, the kids didn't mean the absolute end to life as we knew it—it was the onset of the fifty-hour workweek. Either way, by the time the majority of us blew out the thirtieth candle on the birthday cake, the gig was up. Unless we belonged to the .00005 percent of guys that make the major leagues, we were desperate for competition and an excuse to delay the inevitable. We are all bound by the fact that we entered adulthood kicking and screaming and in search of a game.[2]

---

[2] *I am also working under the assumption that no more than .00005 percent of those playing recreational softball never, ever played baseball. Maybe even .00004 percent!*

That's all I want. A game. A little bit of theater with no known outcome. A healthy dose of competition. Some time with my buddies.

I relish that anticipatory jolt in the morning. Sometime between changing a diaper and letting the dog out—my mornings are all about the feces management, these days, but that's life in suburbia—I smile, realizing that yes indeed, tonight, I've got game. Oh to know that come 6:30 or 7:45 or 9:00, I will be on the field of play . . . I don't care if it's sixty and raining. I don't care if the ump is the opposing pitcher's best friend's uncle. I don't care if my team is 2-10 and has yet to score more than three runs. I don't care if I only get to bat twice. (Well, all right. I do care about *that*.) Just gimme game.

I am fortunate that, despite being a father and having two jobs, I still have time to play. I am fortunate in that I have a place to play and guys to play with. Time, place, guys, the recipe of sweet success.

Three years ago we moved to Madison from New York and I fell in with a bunch of like-minded fellows. These are guys who will get up at 8:00 on a Sunday morning to shoot hoops. They'll get up even earlier to squeeze in eighteen holes before returning home in time for lunch with the family. These are guys willing to risk injury, and reinjury, to line it up between the hash marks on third and ten. Who will leave the house at 11:00 on a Sunday night because that's the only available ice time. Who will scratch and claw their way up the tennis ladder. Who push the office chair *away* from the trash can just to see if they can make it from three-point land. Whose ears perk up at the mere mention of an outing, game, or match. These are men who become boys at the drop of a hat, puck, or putt.

And there are people like this in just about every town across America. Folks who love their children, who love their spouses, their boyfriends, their girlfriends, who love their dogs, cats, and neighbors, but who really, really *love* their games. More so than any other sport, this is a group that loves the national pastime. And at our age, it's baseball if we're watching, softball if we're playing.

It was from my father that I learned to love the game. (Yes, I mist up at the end of *Field of Dreams* and so do you, so lay off!) I played throughout high school, including Februaries in Florida and summers traveling with my Legion team, and then for two more years in college. Mine is the typical tale of an athlete in decline: from high school hero (a stretch) to college zero (the awful truth). Yes, this is the confession of a man who competed at the lowest possible level of collegiate ball. It's true, you simply cannot find a worse brand of baseball than Division III junior varsity. But when, in 1993, I confessed this to Pat Borders before a Blue Jays game, he simply stated that, "Any brand of ball is good ball." Encouraging words from a major leaguer, a World Series MVP no less! And hey, when the Hobart Statesmen made it to their first ever NCAA tournament, I was there. Unfortunately, it was in the booth as the color man for our college radio station, but like I said: I was there!!!

In order to secure your trust in me, I will share one glory day highlight. Pull up a chair, crack open a beer, and get ready to hum some Bruce Springsteen, men. Well, despite all of my collegiate calamities, I was invited to try out for the Cleveland Indians in the spring of 1990. I drove to the field with my dad and you could practically hear the orchestra tuning up to play the score from *Field of Dreams*. And this really *was* a dream come true. The baseballs were so white they glowed. Chief Wahoo adorned every helmet, clipboard, and equipment bag. The scouts wore those too-tight gym coach shorts and carried stopwatches. Their pockets runneth over with pens, whistles, rosters, and tins of Kodiak. This was big time, baby. This was about making it to The Show!!!

I promptly hit the first two batters I faced and soon thereafter all things round, from pizzas to plates, began to look more like softballs and less like baseballs to me. Glory days, well they'll pass you by . . .

In between this tryout and my first slow-pitch softball game with the men of Payne, I did take one last shot at hardball, toeing the rubber with the Newburgh Expos in a semipro league. We only had four or five guys who could pitch and whenever I took the ball for the back end of a doubleheader, I knew that I had to last for all seven innings. There was nobody else left to throw. The walks outnumbered the strikeouts and the losses outnumbered the wins, but I had a blast. At the end of that summer, though, even I had to admit (from a prone position) that pitching myself within an inch of back surgery was a sign not to be ignored. Goodbye baseball, hello pain. Hello Payne.

Payne Environmental was good enough to win the Madison Beach and Rec "B" League championship in 2003, but suspect enough to thwart the obligatory move up to the "A" League for the following season (a bylaw, like so many of the rules of softball, that is rarely adhered to here in town). It's a good thing, too. We got knocked out in the first round of the playoffs this year. We were swept, but as with many of my experiences, I'm just thankful; thankful to be able to say that I was on the field; thankful to be able to say that I'm still playing; even if it is for Payne Environmental at The Surf Club and not for The Tribe at The Jake.

I've always loved sports. And I will always love sports because I'll always love having fun. The brand of ball I'm playing these days, from batting practice with a cooler in shallow left to postgame poppers at the bar, is just fine with me. It's a level that suits my wants and needs perfectly. It's a level that suits my declining skills. But who knows, if I'm feeling daring someday, if the opportunity presents itself, maybe I'll take a shot at fast-pitch . . .

But until then, I'll resign myself to playing slow-pitch and to writing all about it. I imagine that if you're sitting down to read this book, it's probably a cold winter day and you can't wait for spring and you're so desperate for softball that you figured maybe reading would help numb the pain a bit. You can't wait to wake up to a game day and *Softball for Weekend Warriors* is simply serving to bridge the gap. Then again, maybe it's July and you just finished an extra-inning affair and as one *SportsCenter* fades into another you're soaking your ankles and icing your knees, a heating pad on your back and a cold beer in hand. You're reading because you're immobile, but the real reason you're reading is that you want more. Your appetite for the game is insatiable.

Well, congratulations. Whether you're a rookie to the rec leagues or a grizzled veteran, you are a weekend warrior. And you are not alone. We all return to our youth with that most simple of phrases: "Play ball!"

1

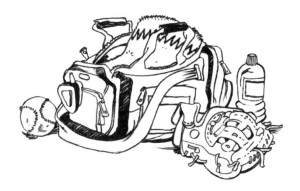

From Slow-Pitch to Sixteen-Inch: Variations of the Game

When we played softball, I'd steal second base, feel guilty, and go back.

—*Woody Allen*

HISTORY OF THE GAME

Admittedly, softball is a kind of pseudo-retirement for me. That being said, it's a sport that many, many people take seriously. It's also the only form of the sport that some have ever known, not having played hardball as a kid. Take a look at any Little League in America and you'll find one or two girls on each team, but look closer and you'll find more and more softball leagues for girls. Starting at a young age, these girls are being prepared for higher levels of competition and maybe even college scholarships.[1] Or so their parents hope!

Not everyone playing softball is soft. There are those who want to continue to compete at the highest level possible. For them, there are men's baseball leagues, but much more common is fast-pitch softball. Although the sport has diversified over the years, all forms of softball share a common history: a link to baseball and an origin in the late nineteenth century . . .

Softball is, according to most definitions, a variant of baseball played with a larger ball on a smaller field. The first version of softball was invented by George Hancock in Chicago in 1887. The game, known as indoor baseball, was played at the Farragut Boat Club. Hancock and friends thought of it as winter baseball, a way to stay in shape and keep in touch with the sport they loved so much. Hancock, a journalist, simply took a boxing glove and tied it tightly so that it more closely resembled a ball. A "soft" ball. Then, not unlike many generations of stickballers, he liberated the handle from the broom and he had a bat. Since the ball was so soft, everyone played barehanded, giving birth to Chicago-style softball. At that point, mitts and gloves were new to baseball anyway, having been used for the first time in 1882.

Word of the sport spread and in 1895 Lewis Rober, Sr., adapted the game to the outdoors as a form of exercise for firefighters in Minneapolis. The league that quickly formed thereafter was known as the Kitten Ball League and the players called the game "kitten ball," perhaps because the ball was soft or maybe because firemen were known for saving curious cats caught up in

---

[1] *Disclaimer: If it seems like I'm not really making an effort to include women in this book, I'm not. Any kind of serious softball transcends the sort of silliness that is most often associated with being a weekend warrior. Plus, I am a man playing in a men's league. On a related note, most of my commentary is also directed towards slow-pitch softball.*

trees. It's all speculation at this point! But back to the details of the game, unlike in Chicago, the firefighter's ball was only twelve inches in circumference. The boys at the Farragut Boat Club were using a sixteen-inch ball, a tradition that still lives in the Windy City today (more on that later). As the years went by, the dimensions of the Farragut field stuck, but the firefighter's ball was preferred.

After spending some time as indoor baseball, kitten ball, mush ball, and diamond ball, the name softball finally stuck— 1926 marked the first use of this name. The Amateur Softball Association was formed in 1933 and finally, a standard set of rules was established to go along with the agreed-upon name.

In 1938, softball reached the ten-million mark for the first time, meaning that one-tenth of the nation's people played at least one game of softball that year. Little did these pioneers know that their game would grow to be *the* number-one participant sport in the United States. According to *The Worth Book of Softball*, ten million more people play softball every year than basketball, thirty million more than soccer! As a matter of fact, in 2003 more than fifty-five million people played in at least one softball game. Cottage industries have blossomed, from websites to equipment manufacturers to books to happy-hour deals. Softball teams have been known to keep local restaurants and bars in business all on their own.

Post-game celebrations are even more fun when the team is co-ed. In terms of happenings on the field, co-ed leagues do pay close attention to fair play. Teams are allowed to have a couple of combinations of players on the field at any time. A team may field five men and five women, five men and four women (in which case the team must alternate gender in the batting order and an out will be awarded whenever two men bat back-to-back; also, if a male batter is walked, the next female batter has the option to take a walk or to bat), four men and five women, or four men and four women. No more than three men may play in the infield at any time. Leagues with these kinds of strict rules tend to be very competitive.

In some co-ed leagues, the setup is more simplistic and the level of play a bit less competitive. Teams simply must have two women in the field and in the lineup at all times. There are no rules regarding infielders or place in the batting order. After a day of work, everybody rushes into the restrooms, slips off their ties and panty hose, pulls on the shorts and T-shirts, and hits the field for a game that tends to be more like happy hour than the Olympics.

One variation of the game is the aforementioned fast-pitch softball, which most closely resembles baseball. The comparisons come with the velocity and movement of the pitches as well as the fact that nine players are used, defensively, on the field. When most people think of softball, though, they think of beer-bellied men lumbering around the bases after smacking a slow, arcing pitch.[2] Slow-pitch softball is a game for the aging, a chance to experience the thrill of victory and the agony of da feet. A favorite of corporate leagues or, in the least, the company picnic, it's a way for friends to haze one another about athletic shortcomings, an excuse to drink beer under the sun. Slow-pitch even sounds nice on the ears. In the summer, things should be a bit slow. Right?

As you can see, there are a number of ways to participate in the nation's number-one participant sport. There are thousands of teams playing in hundreds of leagues. Really, there's something for everyone. Whether it's the casual co-ed corporate league or the most competitive of the softball variants, women's fast-pitch (as seen in the Olympics), there is fun to be had. Good times . . . on small fields . . . with big balls.

[2] *These are the folks I envision when I think of weekend warriors. These are my teammates, my boys. Roll, Payne!!!*

Balls, Bats, Facts, and Stats:

The Amateur Softball Association of America, a nonprofit organization, has more than ninety local associations that register teams and organize leagues all across the country. This includes more than four million players on over 25,000 softball teams. Age of participants ranges from kids in the Junior Olympics to the more than one million seniors playing on masters teams. The ASA was founded in 1933 by Leo Fisher and Michael J. Pauley and was named the national governing body of softball in 1978 by the United States Olympic Committee (USOC).

DETAILS OF THE GAME(S)

No matter what brand you're playing, in softball one constant is that the ball is always pitched underhand. This means that the ball must be released below the hip and that the arm cannot be any further away from the body than an elbow's length. There are no such rules in baseball, but this underhanded aspect applies to both slow and fast-pitch softball.[3]

In slow-pitch softball, a pitched ball must follow an arc whose pinnacle is at least as high as the batter's head but no higher than

---

[3] *Throwing the ball underhanded is a much more natural motion than the overhand contortions of a baseball pitcher. That is why, even in highly competitive fast-pitch softball, pitchers can throw more often than in hardball.*

ten feet, twelve feet, or the height of the backstop (ask somebody on your team to clarify the league's rule). Because of the need to throw the ball in an arc, the pitcher's toss has to come in relatively slow. There is no such restriction in fast-pitch softball, thus the name. In slow-pitch, a pitch may be called illegal if it is higher than the rules allow or if it comes in flat (meaning that the pinnacle is lower than the batter's brow). In order for a strike to be called, the ball must cross the plate between the batter's chest and lower thigh in fast-pitch, armpits and knees in slow. In baseball, the strike zone is supposed to be the same as fast-pitch softball, but the umpires have been squeezing pitchers for years, calling only those pitches that cross home plate between the belly button and knees. Home runs sell tickets. Shutouts do not.

Everybody from hardball to softball, Japan to the Netherlands, knows that four balls means you walk. Three strikes and you're buying the beer. Or at least going back to the bench with a K next to your name in the scorebook.

Some leagues, like the Madison Beach and Rec "B" League, begin each hitter's at-bat with a count of one ball and one strike. This, in an effort to keep the length of the game under an hour and a half. The way our schedule is arranged, there are three games a night with just one hour and fifteen minutes between each start time (6:30, 7:45, and 9:00). At least that's the hope. There are no rules governing the length of our games, but in places with higher demand for the fields, like in urban leagues and parks without lights, chances are there will be some sort of a time limit.

While on the topic of speed, runners in baseball and fast-pitch softball are allowed to steal. In baseball, they may leave the base at any time, but in fast-pitch they have to wait until the ball has left the pitcher's hand. In the majority of slow-pitch leagues, there is no stealing, though it is sometimes considered. Thankfully, the managers in Madison voted it down this past off-season. Unanimously. Some days, the fat man does come out on top!

Although runners cannot steal, they may advance in all of the other traditional manners: on a hit or after another player walks, after a sacrifice fly has been caught (following the regular rules of tagging up until the ball is caught), an error by a fielder, and/or on a balk. I've never seen a balk called in slow-pitch, but I did have the pleasure, once, of seeing a big man run away from a little bee that was buzzing around first base. The base ump told him to either get back to the bag or he was going to be called out. Big Man reluctantly retreated and fortunately for him, the bee had taken flight. The end.

Beware the Buzz!

No, not the buzz of a bee. A beer buzz! One disaster that has befallen many a cerveza-soaked softball team is batting out of order. If you all have been hittin' the sauce before a game, just make sure someone is keeping the book at all times. This concerned bench warmer should announce who the first three batters of the inning are whenever the team comes off the field and everybody should keep an eye on whoever is in the hole—make sure that he really is up next or else your team will be charged with an out.

In most rec leagues, there is a mercy rule that ends the game after the fifth inning if one team is winning by twelve or more runs. Getting mercied sucks. And truth be told, mercying another team sucks. I want to kick dirt from my spot at the hot corner for a full seven innings. I want to get all of my at-bats. I want to play in a competitive game! But sometimes this just can't be avoided, especially during big vacation weeks. Replacement players—like the catcher's cousin, the right fielder's mechanic, the father of the kid I'm tutoring—are recruited, hidden at second or in right-center, and the next thing you know, we're being mercied. To be the final batter in a mercy rule game is the worst. You ground out to short and even though it's only the fifth inning, you have to walk off the field, get your gear out of the dugout so that the next team can enter, and return home an hour before the wife expects you. That means answering a question or two. Ugh.

Ballplayers treasure their time "between the lines." We super-stitious types are sure to never, ever step on those lines when taking the field or leaving it. I am speaking, of course, of the white chalked lines that tell all concerned what is fair territory and what is foul. These lines start at home plate, pass over the outside of the first- and third-base bags and continue out to the foul poles located in the corner of left field and right field.[4] A fence running between the foul poles defines the limits of the field and tempts me every time I'm offered a pitch in the wheel-house!!! In softball, this fence is supposed to be equidistant from home plate at all points, unlike the outfield fence in baseball which is usually farther from home plate in center than down the lines and further still in the power alleys. However, most softball leagues just make use of whatever fields are available. There may be a fence. There may not. There may be a pond, a stand of trees,

---

[4] These foul poles are actually fair poles in that if a ball hits one, it is considered fair and a home run.

a crumbling stone wall, the drive-thru lane of a McDonald's, or just an endless field of grass that forces the runner to kick it into high gear—and keep it in high gear—if he wants that home run. Needless to say, the dimensions of your field were probably determined long ago and without regard for the recommendations of the governing softball body.

Balls, Bats, Facts, and Stats:

In case you're wondering what the ideal is, a regulation softball field has strict rules for its outfield fences. For example, in men's fast-pitch, the fence can be no more than 250 feet from home and no less than 225 feet. Women's fast-pitch has no max, but does have a 200–foot minimum. In women's slow-pitch it is 265 and 275. For men, it is a 275 minimum with no maximum. Coed slow-pitch is supposed to be between 275 and 300 feet from home. Sixteen-inch women's is 200 feet; 250 feet for men. The base paths are also shorter for women, at fifty-five feet. (It is sixty-five feet in slow-pitch and sixty feet in fast-pitch, men and women's alike.)

Home plate is, as in baseball, seventeen inches wide with sides measuring eight and a half inches long before cutting in to meet at the point of the triangle. This point also happens to be where the two baselines, or foul lines, meet. When a slowly pitched pitch in slow-pitch softball (say that ten times fast) lands on the black outline of the sides of home plate, it's called a strike. A slowly pitched softball in slow-pitch softball (nine more times now!) that lands on the white rubber of home plate is called a ball. A slowly pitched softball in slow-pitch softball (OK, even I am willing to admit that this is getting a bit ridiculous now) that hits the batter is laughed at by all and no base is awarded. What kind of a man would take first base after being hit by a slowly pitched softball? Hell, even I don't want to take a base on balls!!!

Home plate is one corner of a sixty-foot square or diamond with bases at each corner. The bases are also square, fifteen inches in length on all sides. They should not be any more than five inches thick, for fear of injury. By the time many of us weekend warriors reach the base, we are ready to tumble in a fit of oxygen-deprived seizures, like a fish in the bottom of the boat. Also, sliding is a dangerous proposition for folks our age. A high-rise of a bag can only add to the danger.

In further efforts to avoid injury, these bases should be secured to the infield. If they aren't, if the bases are loosely tossed onto the field to be kicked around like a bag of shredded Enron documents, write a letter to the league commissioner or town recreation department. Use the word "lawsuit" and they'll act fast enough.

On a related note, beware the slick surface of home plate on rainy days. Step on the front corner, planting the ball of your foot on not much more than the black outside edge unless, of course, you're a fan of falling on your ass in front of family and friends!

And as Matt the Softball Supermodel will tell you, it's important, when playing first base, that you do not put your foot in the middle of the bag when awaiting a throw from an infielder. As the runner, make sure you're stepping on a foot-free bag so that you don't turn an ankle. More on Matt the Softball Supermodel later . . .

Also, be sure to run in foul territory after making contact. Unless, of course, you're trying to get in the way of the catcher's throw after hitting one of those embarrassing swinging bunts that squibs a third of the way up the first-base line. More on that later, too.

Defensively, the infield setup for softball is exactly the same as in baseball with a first baseman, second baseman, shortstop, and third baseman. For the conscientious bench warmer keeping the book, the numbers are the same, too. When scoring, the pitcher is "1," the catcher "2," the first baseman "3," so on and so forth. The outfield is marked by numbers "7" through "10," starting with the left fielder and ending with the right.

The additional outfielder in slow-pitch means that there are four players patrolling the grass. Some teams will employ a "shift" that includes one of the center fielders coming in close to play as more of a shallow center rover. This, in an attempt to cut off those short, bloop-type hits that many veterans have mastered. (It's like they're wielding a tennis racquet, the wily bastards!) Chances are, this rover will play the hitter to pull, standing just to the left of second base for a right-handed hitter; to the right for a left-handed hitter. He may even engage in tomfoolery, lining up to one side and then, as the pitch arcs towards home, sprinting to the other side. Who says it isn't a cerebral game, eh lads?

In fast-pitch softball, the team in the field plays just like in baseball with nine players, including the traditional left, center, and right fielders. In fast-pitch men's softball, the pitcher stands forty-six feet from home plate. For women, the rubber is forty feet from home. There is no pitcher's mound, as in baseball, and the catcher usually wears equipment, although this is rarely the case in slow-pitch. I would recommend a cup for everyone except the outfielders (who might want to sport one, anyway). Say it with me now: "There's nothing wrong with being an athletic supporter." This public service announcement was sponsored by Rawlings, the Softball Widows of America, and our future children.

Demi Moore was an athletic supporter in the classic 1980s flick, *About Last Night*. This is regarded by many to be the greatest softball tribute film of all time, equaled only by the classic confrontation between Bette Midler and George Costanza on TV's *Seinfeld!*[5] All kidding aside, the movie did have its merits, introducing the world to "Chicago-style" sixteen-inch softball. The ball is actually a bit closer to fifteen inches in circumference. Also, it is a bit softer than the regulation softball and a good thing, too, as the players can't wear gloves. As I mentioned before, outside of Hollywood and the Windy City, a softball is approximately twelve inches in circumference (thirty centimeters if you're a fool for the metric system and wish that the Expos had stayed in Montreal). It's larger, softer, and less dense than a baseball. Some years, the balls our league buys seem juiced. Other years, they seem dead. Regardless, I've yet to go yard and am still trying to be as precise as possible with my throws. It's just so much harder for me to grip a softball than a baseball. And remember, I'm the guy who hit two batters at that long-ago tryout. You can imagine how wild some of my throws are, especially when I have to try and nab a speedy runner. Poor Matt, over there at first base.

No matter what the size of the softball, it is made of similar materials the world over. Two pieces of white leather, cut in a figure-eight shape, are sewn together with white thread. (Note: I

---

[5] *According to several Hollywood insiders, Rob Lowe and Jim Belushi did their own stunts. Costanza, too. He had to slide into Midler at home while Belushi had to dry hump a young lady at home after hitting a home run. Belushi had the better agent.*

Matt the Softball Supermodel saves me from yet another error.

say white leather, but some leagues use yellow to increase visibility.) The core of the ball may be made of long fiber kapok, a mixture of cork and rubber, a polyurethane mixture, the heart of a virile lion, or any other approved material.

Softballs are classified by their COR (or "coefficient of restitution"). This is the hardness of a ball as is judged by throwing it against a wall and measuring its rebound speed. The higher the COR, the farther the ball will rebound. Most balls have a COR of 50; this is indicated with blue or white stitching on the ball.

By definition, gloves have fingers while mitts do not. Keeping that in mind, only first basemen and catchers may wear mitts. In most leagues, though, everybody just wears a regular softball glove with the occasional mitt making an appearance.[6] And if you were to poll all of the nation's bat heads (an affectionate term for softball and baseball players alike), I'd be willing

---

[6] To state the obvious, softball gloves are bigger than baseball gloves.

to bet not 10 percent would be able to tell you the difference between a mitt and a glove. I know that despite having a mother who always made sure my hands were warmly ensconced between the months of September and May, I never thought to make the mitt and mitten comparison. Ah, the things we learn.

Different leagues have different rules when it comes to the bat. In general, the approved softball bat may be no more than thirty-four inches long, two and one-quarter inches in diameter, and thirty-eight ounces in weight. While batting and running the bases, women in fast-pitch leagues wear helmets, but men do not.

Balls, Bats, Facts, and Stats:

The first softball league outside the United States was organized in Toronto in 1897. Every four years, the International Softball Federation holds world championship tournaments (in several categories). As of 2004, the defending world champion of men's fast-pitch softball is New Zealand. The defending champ for women is the United States. The US also holds the title for men's slow-pitch. Great Britain is the co-ed champ.

Also on the international front, the USA Softball Women's National Team had their games televised on ESPN twelve times as part of their "Aiming for Athens" pre-Olympic tour. This 2004 television coverage was a record for women's softball.

At the Athens Olympics, the ladies did not disappoint, allowing Australia one run—the only run they gave up for the duration of the tournament—on the way to winning the gold. And there are more future medal winners on the way. The ASA oversees more than 83,000 girls' youth fast-pitch teams, made up of more than 1.2 million girls.

I have touched on a number of different kinds of leagues and some of the rules they might or might not have. Here, in easy-to-read outline form, is an example of some of the more typical rec league rules:

THE RULES IS . . .

1. A twelve-inch softball is used for play.
2. Only official softball bats, approved by the ASA, may be used. No baseball bats are permitted. No tape or any other material may be used more than fifteen inches above the knob of the bat.
3. Ten players are supposed to be out in the field, but you may play with a minimum of eight players. All teams must field their own catcher.[7]
4. Regulation slow-pitch rules are in effect. There are no sidearm or wind-up pitches allowed and the pitcher must face the batter throughout the pitching motion. The arc of the pitch must be a *minimum* of five feet and *maximum* of ten feet. The umpire shall call "Illegal" to acknowledge that the pitch will be called a ball. The batter is allowed to hit a pitch that is not within these limits.

[7] *Meaning this isn't like a sandlot game where the catcher can be borrowed from the other team and there's no hope of a runner getting tagged out at home on a close play.*

5. The horizontal strike zone is determined by home plate; the vertical strike zone is determined by the lines between the knee and armpit of the batter.

6. With two strikes, a batter is permitted to hit one foul ball. However, he is out on the *second* foul ball.

7. The batter must have both feet in the batter's box throughout the swing. No bunting is allowed: the batter must take a full swing. Any half-swing or slap-swing that even remotely resembles a bunt will be called an automatic out.

8. Games shall consist of seven innings, unless the score is tied. Extra innings shall be played until the scheduled start time of the following game or a maximum of three total hours.

9. The Twelve-Run Mercy Rule: If a team is ahead by twelve or more runs after their opponents have batted in the fifth, sixth, or seventh inning, the game is over.

10. All games must begin *within* five minutes of the scheduled game time. If a team is not ready to play by five minutes after the scheduled game time, then a forfeit will be declared.

11. Sliding to "take out" a player will result in an automatic ejection. If there is a play at home plate, third base, or second base, the runner must slide.

12. For safety reasons, players are not permitted to wear metal cleats.

13. Ground rules will be discussed before each game. Both teams must send a representative to home plate when the umpire is ready to review these rules.

14. One base will be awarded to the runner if a live ball goes out of play. The base to be awarded will be determined according to the last base that the runner possessed.

15. All other rules not listed here are as laid out by the American Softball Association. All disagreements are to be decided upon by the league commissioner.

I hate losing. I mean, I love winning, but losing is a much more intense feeling. When I lose, I take it very personally.

—Jennie Finch

2

Weekend Warrior Hall of Fame: Eddie Feigner

Everyone who's anyone has heard of The King and His Court. OK, so maybe you're among the .00005 percent of the population that hasn't. Don't worry: today you shall learn. For starters, let's get one thing straight: Eddie Feigner is The King. Not Elvis. Eddie.

Best known for his fireballing from the rubber, ESPN's David Shoenfield wrote of clocking one of The King's fastballs at an astounding 104 miles per hour! "Sports Illustrated" named his team the eighth most entertaining sports team of the twentieth century. Equally amazing is the fact that The King and His Court have been playing since 1945. In the past fifty-nine years, they have visited over 4,000 cities and according to Bill Dow of *The Detroit Free Press* Feigner has pitched in 11,125 games, thrown 930 no-hitters, and struck out 141,517 batters. Holy cow.

Oh, and did I mention that The Court consists of just four players? There is legend to go along with this fact and legend has it that The Court came to be when Feigner, fresh out of the Marines and playing all across the state of Oregon, challenged a nine-man team to an exhibition game: their nine against his four. There was Feigner toeing the rubber, a catcher behind the plate, a shortstop, and a first baseman. The King lived up to the challenge, throwing a perfect game. The Court won and they're still winning today. All four of them.

Unfortunately, time has taken its toll on Feigner as have two heart attacks, two strokes, and arthritis in both knees. He is also blind in one eye. But none of this stops The King from putting on exhibitions; he is still fond of donning a blindfold and firing strikes from second base. The crowd is also awed when they watch The King do the impossible, like his trick pitches (behind his back, between his legs, etc.).

The team has always been willing to play anywhere, especially in-between doubleheaders of professional baseball games. And there is a good reason for this willingness. When they aren't entertaining military personnel, The Court likes to play for charity. According to their website, they are dedicated to "raising FUN!ds for all charitable organizations with sincere emphasis in our youth and physically challenged programs located within the USA and Canada." That's philanthropy. That's Hall of Fame material!

3

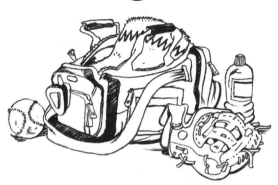

When You Just Don't Have the Skills to Pay the Bills

> I make my weaknesses my strengths, and my strengths stronger.
>
> —Lisa Fernandez

It's hard to believe, but those Indians scouts still can't find my house. The least they could do is call, right? But no, not one message on my cell phone. There's been nothing these past fifteen years, not even a call to my landline. I mean really, it's inexcusable, what with the Internet and all. I have three e-mail addresses and one of them is rightyforhire@cheapballplayer withoutanagent.com! What the heck are they waiting for? *¿Donde esta Chief Wahoo?*

Number-one draft picks come and number-one draft picks go. Sixteen year olds with soft hands and golden guns are plucked from the shores of the Caribbean and inserted into major league infields before they can even love their first woman. Forty-five-year-old lefties prove, time and again, that they have more lives than a cat. Japanese superstars are imported like discounted Hondas then run like souped-up Corvettes. And here I sit, a righty who couldn't break eighty in his prime. The truth hurts.

All right, so we're all in the same boat. Somewhere along the line, it became evident—no matter how deep the denial—that we just didn't have the skills to pay the bills. We were not meant to be on the cover of *Sports Illustrated* or the lead story on *SportsCenter*. We were not meant to marry actresses and pitch deodorant to the masses. That lot in life was for others. In the biz, they call them "the talent." The shortstops. The power hitters. The corn-fed righties. The crafty lefties. The mascots. Those guys are the talent. The cold hard truth is, instead of getting paid, we do the paying. Their salaries, to be exact. They've got the skills. We pay their bills.

But just because we would have been bad professionals doesn't mean that we have to be bad softball players. Nobody wants to overrun the base and put an end to a two-out rally. Nobody wants to throw a rainbow to the catcher, the ball arriving five seconds after the runner has scored and the guy on second now able to advance to third. Nobody wants to cost their team the game.

After resigning ourselves to the Club de Weekend Warrior, some choices have to be made. Most of us don't have that much time for sports, but the least we can do is scrape off the rust so as to be more help than hindrance. It is well within our control to minimize both physical and mental errors. So, why the heck not?

One man represents the effort to always be improving, to staying sharp and having fun. There is only one man who has the smarts, the savvy, the skills, and the looks to aptly represent the softball-playing weekend warriors of America . . .

Matt the Softball Supermodel!

Smooth fielder, strong arm, decent bat, and a direct line to the president should we need more ice for the cooler: that's our Matt.

Matt is the first baseman on my beloved team. He's been here since the beginning, a player who actually worked for Payne Environmental at one time. Or at least dated the secretary. I can't remember. Anyway, he not only represents our team well, I truly believe that he represents the sport well.

Throughout the book, Matt will serve as an example of how to make your way through skill drills and how to stretch, how to work the umps and how to win with class. He saved me at least ten errors this past season and still had it in him to buy a round afterwards, so I figured I owed him a shot at the limelight. His fifteen minutes of fame, right here in this very book.

Matt knows, I know, we all know that quickness is fleeting. It could be that the back keeps locking up on you or it could be that your knees are ready to apply for AARP membership long before you are. They may not even hurt, but chances are your feet have slowed down immensely. Like Fred Flintstone trying to get going, you've got to kick dirt up for a good two or three seconds before forward momentum can carry you toward the ball or base. If you're like Matt and me, you still have juice left in the arm and your bat still has some pop, but it just isn't quite as easy to get to the ball like you used to.

PLAYING SOLID DEFENSE

If you want to go a step beyond stretching and not hurting yourself, keep these pointers in mind. For starters, have your body prepared and ready before every pitch. Don't daydream. Don't get

Matt, ready at first.

so involved in a conversation with the ump or base runner or shortstop that you miss the arc of the pitch and the subsequent frozen rope making its way toward your head. Don't get caught with your pants down. Infielders, bend at the waist and hold not just your glove hand but also your free hand out in front of your body. Like a pulling guard in football, you can throw your arm up and out to get yourself moving to one side or the other.

Outfielders, make sure to have both hands up by your chest and one foot slightly in front of the other. This will either be your push-off foot, for a ball over your head, or your landing foot if you have to start coming in quickly on a ball. Feel free to also keep in mind the physics of the tailing ball: a line drive off of the hitter's bat, be he righty or lefty, will tail towards the foul lines. And sway a little on the balls of your feet before the pitch is delivered because an object in motion tends to stay in motion.

While on clichés . . . The eyes have it. Don't look at your feet. Don't even look a mere five to ten feet in front of you. Look at the batter. Better yet, follow the ball from the pitcher's hand to the point of contact to your glove. If you're an outfielder, run on the balls of your feet to minimize the "bounce effect" (this is when the ball appears to bounce every time your heels hit the ground). Speaking of bounce, if you're an infielder, count the number of bounces as the ball skips towards you. This will help you to focus.

And I know you've been hearing it since your Little League days, but keep your body in front of everything that comes your way. Think of yourself as more of an airplane than a helicopter when it comes to getting down for the ball. You don't want to "land" at the last minute. You want to gently touch down and be in good position by the time the ball arrives. And trust me, after years of playing the hot corner, the balls arrive quickly!

Here's Matt fielding with two hands.

Matt brings the ball up to his chest.

Keep your bare hand above the base of your glove, just in case of a tough hop, and stay down on the ball until it's squarely in your glove. And to make sure that you don't misplay it, as you're coming up bring the ball (in your bare hand) and glove (protecting said ball) in to your belly button before releasing your hand and arm to the throwing position. This guarantees that the ball won't squirt past you or bounce off of a leg.

And in another tribute to your Little League coach, one last little reminder: catch pop flies with two hands. Please. And if someone is on base, catch the ball with the momentum of your body moving towards the infield. Crow hop and throw.[8]

I'm certainly not the only baseball convertee out there, which means I'm not the only one who sometimes struggles with the size of the softball. For starters, a baseball requires a two-finger grip, usually across the seams for guaranteed accuracy. You're now playing with a ball that is nearly twice as large so give it a third finger. (No, not that finger.) That being said, you still want to grip with the fingers and not the palm. There should be daylight between your palm and the ball, no matter what kind of ball you're throwing.

And if you can feel the seams with your three fingertips, all the better. Get your feet under you and throw as overhand as possible.[9] Use your warm-up tosses as an opportunity to practice this. And if you're having trouble, there's no shame in "looking" (remember, the eyes have it) the ball out of your glove. Once it becomes natural, you will be moving the ball even as you pull it

---

[8] *And hit the cutoff man. Somebody in the infield will tell the second baseman or shortstop where to throw it. It's too hard for you to determine from the outfield and too many runners are allowed to advance to scoring position because of misguided throws. On the other hand, there is no greater feeling than gunning someone down at home!!!*

[9] *Make sure that your throwing elbow is always higher than the throwing shoulder. Otherwise, the ball is sure to banana away from the infielder and all of a sudden your team is looking like the Bad News Bears!*

Matt demonstrates the three-finger grip on the ball, with spacing.

Matt demonstrates the three-finger grip on his beer, with spacing.

out of your glove and will have it well held by the time you cock to throw.

Keep in mind that once your arm starts coming forward, the cocking is over. Your wrist should be loosey-goosey. Snap that wrist towards the target and the velocity will be there.

In order to better ensure an accurate throw, don't square your body to the intended target. Squaring is for when you catch the ball, but you now need to get your body behind the throw. So, turn sideways in preparation. By turning, you are sure to have your feet beneath you just as you are sure to avoid being lazy and throwing flat-footed and sidearm. You'll lead with the opposite foot and you'll stay on the balls of your feet, got it? Good. Now, remember all the other basics like to hit your target in the chest and then follow through. Don't rush, either. The only thing worse than letting someone get on base is letting them take the *extra* base on an errant throw.

Before shifting gears, another public service announcement: keep in mind that stretching and warming up is of the utmost importance. More on that topic to follow.

Also to follow are some pointers on giving the business to the umpires, but for now let's make their job as easy as possible. In particular, if you're the fielder involved in a bang-bang play, do all that you can to make sure the umpire can see the play (and call the runner "Ouuuuuuuut!!!"). The first thing an infielder needs to do is set up to receive the throw. Naturally, you want your body to be as close to the outfielder as possible. If you're at second base and the throw is coming in from right field, you will be on the outfield side of the bag, right behind it with your glove stretched out towards right. Assumedly, you're a righty, so your body will be facing first base with your head turned left so as to watch the throw come in. The runner is bearing down on you but since you're facing him, as soon as you catch the ball, you can

Joe demonstrates the sweep tag.

sweep tag, looking to slap his sliding foot before it can make contact with the bag. Now, the part about helping the umpire . . .

The sweep tag is used so as to get the mitt down as quickly as possible. It's also used to show the ball to the umpire after the tag has been made. All good umps will wait to make sure the ball hasn't been knocked free before signaling an out. As soon as the umpire sees your raised glove with the ball still inside, the call will be made. Now, all you have to do is call time out (to ensure that all other base runners stay put) and get the ball back to the pitcher. Or, throw it around the horn if no one's left on base.

If possible, though, a two-handed tag is best. Like catching a pop fly, this is the safest way of making sure that you hold onto the ball. It also enables you to block the base, if you have the time. Put your foot between the sliding foot of the base runner and the bag. Just keep the blocking leg loose so there's some give when the runner makes contact. You want to keep him from getting to the bag, but not at the expense of your knee. If

Joe demonstrates the two-handed tag.

there isn't time to get your body between foot and bag, just do it with your glove.

Another fundamentally sound play for infielders is looking the runner back. When a runner is in scoring position—meaning second or third base—and a ground ball is hit to the left side before the throw is made to first, the shortstop or third baseman should look the runner back. Why let the runner advance a base if you can keep him where he is and still get the runner out at first? As you crow hop, give a look, then refocus on first and fire!

On hot shots that are sure to make it to the outfield, an infielder may also delay the advance of the base runner by pretending to have a play on the ball. Sell it like a quarterback on a play-action pass. While running to the cutoff position or to cover the bag that you're responsible for, if you are anywhere near the vicinity of the ball make it look like you have a shot at it. The runner will hopefully stutter step and have to stop at third rather than attempt to go home.

The fake is especially important in the outfield. On a ball that's dropping before you can reach it, why not jog in with the glove up? Make it look like you're going to catch the ball. The base runner might just tag up rather than advance at full speed. You might just be able to hold him where he is if the hit is shallow enough. In the least, you might very well keep him from rounding third and coming home.

Back to infielders, and in particular cutoff men, for a moment. Someone—either the catcher or the pitcher—will direct the cutoff man as to where to throw the ball and also whether or not they should cut the ball off. If you're told to let the ball go through—let's say to home plate to let the catcher try and make a play on a potential scoring run—why not put the glove up as if you are going to cut the ball off? This may keep the batter at first base. The risk of throwing through (meaning to home plate) is letting the other base runners advance. Do what you can to keep them where they are. It might be what (finally!) puts an end to the rally.

In the ongoing effort to have a fundamentally sound softball team, make sure that people back up the bases that they're supposed to back up. If nobody is on base, the catcher should back up first on a ground ball, especially if there is no fence to contain a rebellious throw. Fortunately for us, Johnny Cat is quick like a cat (thus the name) and hustles down the line to back Matt up. Otherwise, the batter gets second. If the pitcher is not being used as a cutoff man, then he should be behind third base or home plate if there's even a remote chance of a play. And the left fielder has nothing to do on a ground ball to right. Unless, of course, there's going to be a throw to third base to try to get a runner. If the potential exists, then that left fielder needs to haul ass and back up the bag. And with two center fielders, there's no reason why, on a swinging bunt with a runner at first, both men shouldn't be breaking in towards second in case the pitcher or catcher throws the ball away while trying to force out the lead runner.[10] Get behind second base, pronto.

And although I am a third baseman, I have to rat out my fellow infielders. We don't get to every ground ball. Even the ones hit straight at us can sometimes be an adventure. Right through the wickets! Through the five hole! Easily, the most embarrassing play in all of softball. If you're out in the outfield and you see a hot shot skipping across the dried out dirt of the infield, start breaking in. Just in case one of my fellow infielders is prepping for a bullfight. Olé!

In the prelude I alluded to my favorite play, the pickle. What could be more fun than chasing a runner back and forth, back and forth? If you're an outfielder, get in on the fun while the gettin's good! Not only might your services be needed for the catch-run-throw-catch-run-throw, another set of eyes never hurts, especially if there's a runner on third. Let the fielder with the ball know when that runner starts breaking for home.

A warning for both infielders and outfielders: if there is a runner on base and the batter hits a foul ball when he already has two strikes, don't catch the *next* foul ball, especially if it's hit deep in the outfield and might enable that runner to score. In most leagues, the second foul ball means that the batter is automatically out. Why run the risk of letting a runner tag up and trot home?

There are plenty of books full of drills if you really want to work on your game. I would say, first and foremost, you have to start by being in some semblance of shape.[11] Mobility leaves us almost as quickly as muscle mass. It's tough to run with a beer belly, let alone bend over, field the ball cleanly, and come up

---

[10] *If my beloved Mariano Rivera could throw the ball away, I'm guessing your pitcher is capable, too . . .*

[11] *Yes, I realize that round is a shape. I said "of shape" though, not "a shape!"*

firin'! Softball can be fun, but if you really care about winning, you'd better do something to better guarantee that happens. Spend some time on your footwork, shed a couple of pounds (like ten or twenty), think of what you have to do before every pitch, and play sound defense.

Now, to the other side. The fun side. Hitting!

If you can only do one thing, if you only have a half an hour, sometime in early April before the season gets underway, do this: go to the batting cages and work on driving the ball to the opposite field. Most of us are right-handed. And as right-handed hitters, if we're going to hit behind the runner, we have to learn how to hit to right field. Opposite field.

It's fundamentally sound to punch the ball through the right side so that it will be behind the runner as he approaches second base. Runners have a much better chance of making it to third base if the ball is in right field rather than in left. Watch Derek Jeter to learn all about the inside-out swing; this is one method of hitting the ball to the opposite field. You drag the bat through the zone, keep the hands in tight, and then flick the wrists just before contact, extending the arms at the same time. Think of snapping a towel (just a forehand motion instead of a backhand). And think of keeping your head on the ball and your front shoulder closed. You can step towards right field, but if you open up the upper half of your body, all is lost.

In a regular hitting situation, you should always look to hit "through the box" (i.e., right up the middle). Split the center fielders or at least the two middle infielders and your single is virtually guaranteed. It's also easier to adjust to an outside pitch (go with the pitch!) or to pull something nice and meaty on the inside half of the plate. Careful of the setup, however. Smart pitchers will put the ball in a spot just good enough for you to swing full-force and fly out to the left fielder. Don't fall for it!

Matt in his batting stance.

Contact! A nice level swing . . .

Soft-toss.

If you don't have a batting cage nearby, convince a couple of guys to get together for batting practice. In the least, talk one of your loved ones into pitching you some soft-toss (they take a knee at a forty-five degree angle from you and underhand the ball, which you hit against a screen if it's a ball, the side of the house if it's a sock).

Hitting is the most fun part of softball and so, in an ode to offense, here is an original, instructive poem, for you, my fellow weekend warrior.

"Sonnet 69: My Heart Bursteth with Joy Whence Smacking the Crap Out of the Ball"

Put most of your weight on the balls of your feet.
Swing from the heels and you're gonna get beat.
Your feet should be spaced shoulder-width apart.
For breakfast I ate a strawberry Pop Tart.

Your front shoulder low and cocked inwards so slightly.
Greet the pitcher with a finger, held aloft impolitely.
Short stride when swinging, be under control.
Scout out the fielders and look for the hole.
Keep the hips closed, the barrel of the bat above your hands.
Hitting up the middle should be in your plans.
The knob of the bat must lead that barrel.
Stroke like Viagra and not like you're sterile.
Your wrists should roll as you release those hips.
Sour cream and onion is the king of all dips.
Aim chin, chest, and trouser snake at the point of contact.
In your trot, tell the shortstop 'bout your big money contract!

And now, a poem for those mired in a slump. Oh, unrequited love. Oh, fading glory . . .

"Roses Are Red, Your Hitting Makes Me Blue"

If you're overstriding, don't even take a step.
Stop stepping in the bucket, quit being a schlep.
If you're opening up, tell your front shoulder "Behave!"
Keep back as long as possible, then surge forth like a wave.
If you're uppercutting, the answer is clear.
Chop down like a tree and relax with a beer.
If you're not seeing the ball well, then open your stance.
Slide the front foot out slightly, be smooth like Jim Nantz.
If you're pulling pop flies every time at the plate.
Forget about the homer, a single's your fate.

Even if you're the worst hitter on your team, you can still contribute. When you're waiting on deck, act like a base coach if there's a play at home plate. Help your teammate out by yelling

When slumping, sometimes all it takes is a swinging bunt of a hit to break you out of your malaise. Not mayonnaise, fool. Malaise!

"Up!" or "Down!" You've got to let the runner know if he has to slide because of an incoming throw ("Down!") or if he can stay up and avoid shredding some skin ("Up!"). Then, get up yourself and drive somebody in!

Batting cages have gotten a bit pricey in recent years, but it's not going to be any more than ten bucks and, at most, a half an hour of your time. Besides, it's all in how you approach the "workout." Think of it as a chance to have some fun and knock out the cobwebs. Keep in mind that, like anything else, softball can be an expensive and time-consuming sport, depending on how seriously you take it. But, more often than not, softball requires no more than a minimal league fee (field maintenance, lights, and umpire's salaries). Splurge a little and get that new jock strap and who knows? Maybe Santa will come through for once and slip the latest "Wonderboy" from DeMarini or Easton under your tree.

If you do spend a little bit of cash on the game, I can't help but feel that it's money well spent. But if further justification is needed, the following is a list of some of the stupid things that men—yes, even some of us weekend warriors—have been known to pull the credit card out for:

THE STUPID EXPENDITURE LIST

1. Double decaf latte
2. Purebred dog
3. New driver (with oversized head)
4. Subscription to GQ, Men's Journal, or Good Housekeeping
5. Carb-free (i.e., cardboard) snack bars
6. Those "14 CDs for a Penny!" music clubs
7. Internet porn
8. Air Jordans
9. Turducken
10. Hair implants
11. Craps at the San Soprano Festival

Although I will admit to moments of insanity—vintage Air Jordans, both CD clubs, the craps, and the Turducken—I know that if the expense of playing is justifiable on my teacher's salary, there's got to be a way for you to spin it. Really, I would say that I spend, at most, $250 every season. Everybody on our team gives $25 to Neal Payne (a little thank-you for his sponsorship and the uniforms); I spend another $25 on Gatorade, bananas, and Advil; and the other $200 goes towards bar tabs and barbecues.

If you're still worried, you can always ask your teammates for help. Someone's liable to have an old jock they can lend you.

4

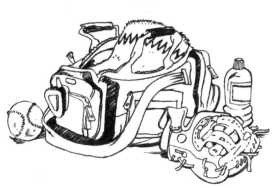

Weekend Warrior Hall of Fame: Ty Stofflet

Ty Stofflet, a left-handed pitcher hailing from Coplay, Pennsylvania, was inducted in the ASA Hall of Fame in 2004. For forty-plus years he was one of the nation's premier fast-pitch pitchers. His 46-20 record in sixteen national fast-pitch championships is the second best, all-time. He was named MVP of that tournament five different times and was named an ASA All-American ten times. And how about these numbers? 1,500 victories, 650 shutouts, 172 no hitters, and 58 perfect games. Eye popping.

Ty played for a number of teams over the years. These included several contenders for the aforementioned national championships. There was the Patriots Club of Allentown, Sal's Lunch of Philadelphia, and both the Rising Sun Hotel and Billard

Barbell of Reading.[12] Ty played until he was fifty-nine years old, lengthening a legend already aided by all the trophies and an article in *Sports Illustrated*.

Ty was amongst a class of seven to be inducted during the 2004 ASA National Council meeting in Orlando. Of note is fellow Hall of Fame inductee, Emily Alexander of Phoenix, Arizona. Emily was recognized for her years of service as an umpire; she is the thirtieth umpire to be inducted, but the first woman. See? We weekend warriors are willing to recognize good work from Blue. Man, woman, or child, who cares? Just call a good game!

Dubbed "The fastest pitcher in America" by *The New York Times* on August 11, 1985, Ty Stofflet is now the subject of a biography. If your interest has been piqued, *Softball's Lefty Legend: Ty Stofflet*, by Steven Clarfield, is now available. Read more about a real living legend.

---

[12] *I just love rec league team names, starting with my all-time favorite, Chico's Bail Bonds!*

5

"But honey, look . . . I'm losin' weight!"

Here now, a gift from that most revered of weekend warriors, the king of kite-flying himself, Benjamin Franklin. It is a maxim for us all to live by: Money spent on sport is money well spent.

OK, so that one didn't really appear in *Poor Richard's Almanac*. And yes, I admit it, I made the whole thing up. But let's not kill the messenger here. It's true, isn't it? Money spent on sport *is* money well spent.

For most weekend warriors, whether or not we can get out to play has little to do with disposable income. The issue is actually sneaking away from our responsibilities for a couple of hours. It can be a yeoman's effort just to get out of the house or the office to play a game. My league runs from April to July and we generally have games two nights a week. Three times during the season, however, we have an additional game on Friday night. Not that I needed to do much smoothing over, but in our house there are two running lists: the grocery list and the shit list. And trust me, you don't want to be on the shit list.

So, just to make sure that none of us ended up on a loved one's shit list, the brain trust that is Payne Environmental agreed to turn those Friday night games into . . . (drum roll, please) . . . a family outing. There was dining à la charcoal. There was chardonnay for the ladies. Pleasantries were exchanged as we took turns pushing each other's children on the swings. The sun slowly set on Long Island Sound, eventually the lights came on, and the kiddies went home to bed. Game time.

As a friend once told me, "I'd rather beg for forgiveness than ask for permission."[13] But really, honesty is the best policy and so I recommend being as upfront as possible with both the boss *and* the wife. That being said, if there's a 6:30 game and an ego at your place of employment needs to be soothed or an angry better half at home needs to be placated, you'd better put on that thinking cap. Do not overestimate the power of the little white lie.

One of the more foolproof justifications is your health. As winter wears on, I know that I tend to get a little, shall we say, portly. Despite pickup basketball twice a week, my body builds blubber like Henry Ford built cars. The snacks flow my way as if the little elves at Keebler are doing double-time on the assembly line! From holiday hors d'oeuvres to the Super Bowl spread to the feeding frenzy that is March Madness, I do some mighty, mighty eating. Needless to say, when the calls start coming in and there's talk of "throwing the pill" and "shagging some flies," I simply point to the love handles and mention my high cholesterol. The missus nods skeptically and away I go!

---

[13] *Actually, several friends now that I think about it. Does that mean it qualifies as a Franklinesque maxim?*

Oh to be running after a long winter's rest, zigzagging through freshly cut grass with a glove on one hand and a beer in the other.

I mean . . . Oh to be tracking a low liner, snagging it before it touches the ground and following it up with nine solid cuts (I get ten swings, but insist on bunting the first pitch, just for old time's sake). What a beautiful thing to be shagging balls in mid-April. What a blast to be blasting away from the batter's box. How good it feels to be exercising out in the great outdoors once again.

Each swing, each throw, each ray of sunshine—with each I can practically feel the pounds melting away!!!

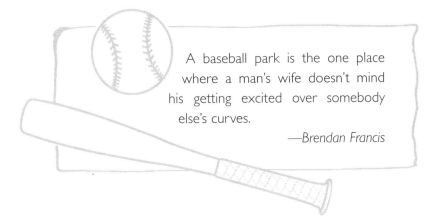

A baseball park is the one place where a man's wife doesn't mind his getting excited over somebody else's curves.

—Brendan Francis

On that note, I cannot stress enough how well the weight excuse can work during the season, just so long as you don't overdo it. Not the excuse making. I mean the eating! Make sure that all those pregame beers and postgame calamari don't start showing. Midseason acquisitions have propelled many a team on their championship run. Just make sure your midseason acquisition isn't a double chin. If softball season means you *gain* five or ten pounds, you're screwed. You must, I repeat, you MUST be able to say, "But honey, look . . . I'm losin' weight!"

And it's something we're all aiming to achieve anyway: a little bit of competition and a good report from the doctor.[14] This is why the excuses qualify as nothing worse than little white lies. If you were sneaking off to lose the mortgage at Texas Hold'em, now that might go down as a *bold-faced* lie. But to get out for a game . . . The pearly gates will still open wide for you when the time comes, my friend. Just be wise, otherwise the wife is liable to ship you up to see St. Pete long before your time. Either that or you'll be given a permanent spot on her shit list.

Speaking of getting yourself in trouble, be very careful at work. I've heard tales of softball-induced divorce, but I suspect job performance has suffered equally. My advice: save your "Get Out of Jail Free" cards for when you really need them. If it's a 6:30 game in May, you might have to sacrifice a little. Essentially, you're losing the battle in order to win the war. A playoff game in late July is far more worthy of your fictions: the end-of-the-day dentist appointment, picking up a sick child from day care, car troubles, a tornado that touched down in your backyard and your backyard alone.

But, back in the real world once more, the best you can hope for is to arrive at the field in time to get changed and stretched out. Stretching is of the utmost importance, so much so that I have dedicated a whole chapter to it ("Gluteus Maximus" is coming up next). Really, though, one of the toughest things about being a weekend warrior is switching gears at the drop of a hat. Or, more precisely, the flip of a coin. If you can't convince the boss to unlock your chain a little early and you show up at 6:29 just in time to learn that you're the home team, it means that you have less than sixty seconds to throw on your jersey, tie the cleats, trot out to right field, and rush a warm-up toss or two. And

---

[14] All kidding aside, I highly recommend the annual physical, even if it means you have to sing "Moon River."

you just know that the first hit is headed in your direction because that's the way things work in the predictable world of weekend warrior sports. But who cares? You're on the field. And hopefully you'll still have your job in the morning. A place to sleep that night, too!

Just to lend a helping hand to you, my fellow weekend warrior, here are some excuses I've stored away in the ol' mental Rolodex. Feel free to embellish, at will.

EXCUSES FOR GOING TO A PRESEASON PRACTICE

1. "You see, the younger guys on the team kinda look up to me."
2. "One of the fellas knows a personal trainer and this guy is gonna show us how to get abs like Brad Pitt."
3. "Whoever shows up first gets a gift certificate to The Gap!"
4. "I'm beginning to think Scott Peterson might be innocent . . . "
5. "If I can bat over .500 this year, the boss said he'll give me a $10,000 bonus."
6. "I have marks from the couch branded into my ass. I think it's time I venture outside the TV room, don't you?"

EXCUSES FOR GOING OUT FOR POSTGAME CALAMARI AND BEERS

1. "Delicious and nutritious!"
2. "A recent study found that drinking beer and eating circular fried foods like onion rings and calamari helps to unclog arteries, build muscle mass, and raise the IQ. No, really. I read it!"
3. "I'm afraid they'll talk about me behind my back if I'm not there. Wah."

Matt demonstrates the three-finger grip on a nice piece o' calamari. With spacing!

4. "You won't have to listen to my snoring because you'll already be asleep by the time I get home."

5. "I heard that male bonding helps fight premature balding."

6. "I want to sample their food before I bring you there, sweetheart."

Careful if you do embellish, however. As men, we are the duller of the two sexes. Just remember these two simple things when employing the little white lie: one, don't get cocky. Cocky is not cute and cocky will raise suspicion. Second, more likely than not she already knows the truth. Just be smart and nice about it and you might be pleasantly surprised by how accommodating she'll be. There's nothing less appealing than a chubby hubby and nothing more appealing than the responsible boy. At least that's what I'm banking on when I make the call to her between the field and the bar. It never hurts to have a fact at the ready, too. Something you didn't share before but need now, just for that final convincing note before saying "Good night" and

"You complete me." For example: "Of course I'm going. I saw on the news that four out of five dentists surveyed agree: softball is the nation's number-one weapon against obesity!" She'll giggle, tell you to drive safe, and then the night is yours. Well done!

On the other hand, sometimes you will have no choice but to miss a game. It may be vacation, eviction, conviction, or a half-off sale at the Barcalounger Outlet.[15] In the effort to keep everybody happy, feel free to indulge on one of these . . .

TOP FIVE THINGS TO SAY WHEN YOU'VE GOT TO SKIP A GAME

5. "I've got to babysit my kids, the neighbor's kids, my sister's kids, and those kids who've gone unclaimed since our last barbecue."

4. "Tuesday? Tuesday?! I thought the game was Thursday . . . "

3. "I'll make it up to you all next game with beer, chips, salsa, peanuts, and hookers. You heard me right. I said salsa. On me!"

2. "I'm dying of a rare disease and the only way I'll live is if I spend the week in Jersey with my in-laws."

1. "I don't like softball and I don't like you. See you Thursday."

---

[15] *Did you know that there is a brand of recliner called Klein & Assmann? I'm not making it up. Google it for yourself, Assman!*

6

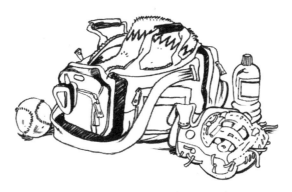

Gluteus Maximus and Other Muscles Just Waiting to Be Pulled

It is common knowledge now that you should warm up the body before undertaking any form of exercise. This has the effect of preparing the heart, muscles, and joints.

—Kelvin Juba

Of the many things that Matt the Softball Supermodel does well, probably the most important is keeping his body parts from breaking down. He's no marathon runner and rarely does he lift a weight, unless, of course, you're willing to count the twelve-ounce curls. No, Matt's specialty is keeping himself limber and off of the disabled list. He's big on stretching and staying loose. Really, when he isn't draining the cooler or smokin' butts, Matt is the picture of health. I myself am not a smoker, but if it helps him to stay steady for my errant throws, so be it. I'll buy the next carton of cancer sticks.

Matt tends to the tender knee.

Matt may be a supermodel, but he's also a regular kind of guy. Responsible but fun, sarcastic and smart, plays with passion but not reckless abandon—knee surgery will do that to you. Thus, the attention he pays to his legs. Also, I mentioned those throws that only make it four-fifths of the way to first . . . Matt knows well enough to get his groin and back ready for the acrobatic feats required to reel 'em in. Glove work is not the problem; it's contorting like a hockey goalie to catch the ball or at least keep it from scooting by for a ground-rule double.

So, follow my advice and follow Matt's example. Here is his stretching routine, in photo essay format.

Straining a groin is the worst. Take your time with the butterfly and life in your pants will be happy, happy, happy.

Must . . . get . . . to . . . Heidi! Yes, it's the mountain climber. Keep those legs and your lower back limber.

The hurdler stretch accomplishes the same, minus Heidi.

Your throwing arm deserves this kind of treatment. And if there's time, treat both arms.

This kind of treatment, too. (Both arm stretches should be revisited at least once during the game.)

Everyone's favorite, it's the all-over body stretch!!!

Warm-up tosses are exactly what you'd expect, outside of the occasional appearance of . . . a football! But Joe isn't just getting ready for fall: the throwing motions are similar and do wonders for shaking the rust off of your cannon.[16]

All kidding aside, stretching is the most important thing you can do if you care to enjoy more than just that first afternoon of shagging flies. In basketball, your body warms up as you're shooting around. And then, the running is sustained: a constant, or at least a semi-constant depending on how winded you get. In softball, the sudden starts can kill you. For the past two innings you've been counting dandelions in right field. Your legs haven't moved at more than a snail's pace since the last game, six days before. Then, all of a sudden, you're swinging like Sammy Sosa but the ball is traveling less like a Waverly-bound bomb and more like a putt. It's the classic swinging bunt and now you've got to haul ass down the line, hoping to save a little face and put off, for as long as possible, a return to the bench where your friendly

---

[16] *And for reminding you of proper, over-the-top mechanics.*

neighborhood cannibals are lining up to eat their own. Think about it: if your car can't go zero to sixty in two seconds, what makes you think you'll be able to?

Simply put, warming up increases the temperature of the muscles so that they can contract and relax more quickly. It also raises—gradually rather than *traumatically*—the heart rate, loosens the connective tissue, and triggers the release of fluid that promotes the smooth movement of bone over bone. Get a load of med-school me.

Forget to stretch before—I also recommend doing some minor stretching and jogging-in-place between innings—and you're destined to snap the guitar string. Anyone who's ever pulled a hammy knows what I'm talking about. It's a twang to beat the band. Immediately, you know that you're going to not only be out of commission for a while, but that everybody at the office is going to look at you funny the next day. The next several days. When you get home, your wife will smirk and your children will show absolutely no mercy. They still want to be picked up and, even worse, chased. Your mother will scold you and your grandmother will call you an idiot. Or vice versa. And all because you couldn't take a minute to stretch.

With my herniated L5S1 disc, I spend a little more time trying to achieve elasticity, but Matt is able to get the lead out in three or four minutes. And that's including his warm-up tosses. But let's say it's one of those hell days at work and you forgot the jersey at home. (Hint: keep an equipment bag in your car at all times.) You're pleased to see there's no traffic, but when you arrive at the house the kids want you to sit with them while they eat. You just can't deny their pleading eyes, let alone the foreboding look your wife gave when you came in. So, you sit. And you watch the clock. And you begin to sweat. To save time, you decide to change right there, in front of your family. Not what anyone wants to see while they dine. No, sir. But for the love of the game, you'll risk scarring your kids for life. It's 6:20 . . .

Kisses all around and then you're off to the park. You arrive with a minute to spare. Your team is on the field first, so you have just one minute to stretch. In the never-ending effort to avoid the disabled list here's what I recommend:

THE ONE-MINUTE STRETCHING ROUTINE FOR OLD BASTARDS

1. **Touching the toes thrice is nice.** You've been doing this since your gym teacher first tested you for scoliosis. Now, bend and touch those toes. Or at least your shins. Don't bounce; hold the position for five seconds and then come back up slowly. Slooowly. Three times, please.

2. **On your back, Jack!** Pull those knees in to your chest and hold for ten seconds. Feel those hammies unwind. Do this twice and then back onto your feet. Up! Up! Up! The umpire has a dinner date and your team is taking the field.

3. **To avoid harm, pull your arm.** Pull your throwing arm across your chest by pinning it between your chest and the inner elbow of your other arm. (Remember the photo?) Alternate this with the other arm stretch: pull your throwing arm over its shoulder so as to further loosen up that nagging tricep. Hold the elbow of your throwing arm in the palm of your glove and push back. Do this between pitches. And until you've done so, do not throw the ball, at least not too, too hard. Remember, my fellow weekend warriors, there is no such thing as an insta-warm-up! Soft-toss with the center fielder until you feel that golden gun loosen up. The last thing you want is to still be tight when the leadoff hitter

tests you. Make sure your arm is more like spaghetti on the plate than spaghetti in the box and throw that bozo out at second!!!

And here's some advice: If you show up at 6:29 and are still feeling tight from the previous game, you might want to let the guy who's been there since 6:00 start in your place. It rewards him his diligence and might save you some pain. The weekend warrior never wants to be on the bench, but three innings might be worth three weeks lost to injury. Besides, who wants to be hazed by their boss? Or worse, scolded by their mother, wife, and children? Nobody. Nooooobody!

Caveat: the advice I just shared is advice I've never followed myself. (I just thought I'd better include that here, lest any of my teammates stumble across this book and think me insincere.) If I'm at the park, I'm in the game. No ifs, ands, or butts.

Now, in the continued effort to save you from those matriarchal decrees, I've got some more health advice. That's right: 215 pounds, on Lipitor, and with a soft spot for melted cheese, and I'm going to get preacherly and teacherly on you. In their book, *Take Care of Yourself*, Donald Vickery and James Fries—mmmmm, fries—make some recommendations and I couldn't agree with them more. For one, have your blood pressure checked every year. Make sure the ol' ticker doesn't rev too high when going from first to third. It's also important that your heart be able to return to resting rate as quickly as possible. For more on this, talk to someone who didn't get a 67 percent in biology and who has a couple of diplomas on the wall (written in Latin and not Crayon).

Speaking of the heart and Lipitor, this just in: bad cholesterol is bad while good cholesterol is . . . You get the point. Although Misters Vickery and French fries recommend getting your cholesterol tested every five years, I'm going to err on the side of caution and suggest you do it annually. This is especially important if you: 1) have an unusually high level of bad cholesterol; 2) have a family history of high cholesterol and/or heart attacks; and 3) if you are a legend in the league for once eating an entire blooming onion.

Misters French fries and Vickery both know that you can't hit a softball if you can't see it. Therefore, they also recommend getting tested for glaucoma. I'm only thirty-three and my doctor is sending me to see the eye doctor. The man is overly cautious, but I'll take it. I may not be a biologist or an optometrist, but I know one thing for sure. It's tough to catch the ball when you can't see it. It's tough to man the hot corner from six feet under.

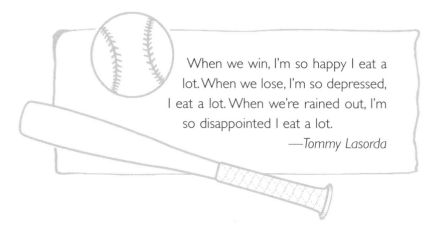

> When we win, I'm so happy I eat a lot. When we lose, I'm so depressed, I eat a lot. When we're rained out, I'm so disappointed I eat a lot.
>
> —*Tommy Lasorda*

Back in college, we used to declare that "moderation is best in all things" before consuming a dozen buffalo wings and a twelve-pack each, plus some mozzarella sticks for dessert. We were a Richard Simmons nightmare. The phrase "freshman fifteen" was wasted on us. I gained the freshman thirty![17] Casual restraint is

---

[17] *Playing baseball sophomore and junior year was a lifesaver. I might not have impressed those Indians scouts, but I did drop the love handles. At least for a while.*

best and this is advice that Misters French fries and Vickery share wholeheartedly. Forget about cold turkey and cutting carbs. Moderation is the way to go. Pass the bleu cheese.

Dr. Atkins never batted above .300 and almost as damning is the fact that so many nutritionists question his philosophy.

"Carbs are to your body what gas is to a car," writes Susan Kleiner in her book *High-Performance Nutrition*. "The major role of carbohydrates in nutrition is to provide energy. During exercise, carbohydrates are one of your main sources of energy."

And why is this energy so necessary? To be able to go from first to third, sure, but even more so, to fight myoatrophy. Between the ages of twenty and seventy, you may lose up to 20 percent of your muscle mass. The change is more dramatic in men than in women and the health consequences can be serious. This is true for even the healthiest of people. But by eating right and staying physically active, especially if you maintain a routine of strength training, the effects of myoatrophy can be minimized. There are so many reasons to stay active—from contributing on the field of play to living longer to staying strong and independent—that it might seem amazing to some that we should even need to be reminded of these things. But we all forget. We are all swayed by that bacon, egg, and cheese; that Carvel ice cream cake. Eat the cake, but skip the second BE&C. Go for a long walk. Throw the ball with your nephew or neighbor.

There are carbs and then there are calories. Everybody agrees, controlling your caloric intake is a pretty good idea. To be specific, it's important to remember that as you lose muscle, your metabolic rate slows down, which means you will not burn off calories as quickly as you once did. We run like rabbits as kids, but trudge like turtles as adults. Obesity is a real threat and being overweight often leads to heart disease, high blood pressure, diabetes, and other such badass diseases. Diabetes is now one of the leading causes of death in the US. As we get older, our bodies lose the ability to regulate glucose and this can lead to adult onset, or Type II, diabetes. Fat ain't phat and that's that.

Kleiner writes, "Maintaining muscle tissue helps normalize the flow of glucose from the blood into muscle cells where it can be properly used for energy."

Carbs . . . Calories . . . Cholesterol . . . So much to worry about, so little time. My answer is: don't worry about it. Like Phil Knight says, "Just do it!" Once you've made a life change, all of the requirements become second nature. Avoiding bad cholesterol *needs* to become natural because news flash: the body produces plenty of it without your help!!!

Eating food that is high in saturated fats and neglecting to exercise are two ways to guarantee high cholesterol levels, especially LDL, otherwise known as "bad cholesterol." This leads to clogged arteries and clogged arteries lead to heart attacks and heart attacks lead to death and death leads to no more doubleheaders. Capisce?

Also, think fiber. Not only will eating foods rich in fiber make you regular (yee ha!), these foods are necessary to avoid the plague. All right, not the plague, but the following list of no-no's are best fought off with a healthy diet heavy in fiber: appendicitis, cardiovascular disease, erectile dysfunction (ouch), colorectal cancer, constipation (ugh), cavities and gum disease, kidney stones and gallstones, hemorrhoids (oy), hernias, high blood pressure, high cholesterol, heart disease, and ulcers (say goodbye to Hooters).

> ### EAT THIS STUFF SO THAT YOU CAN HAVE THE OCCASIONAL CALAMARI
>
> - Bananas, apples, oranges, strawberries, peaches, apricots, prunes, and pears
> - Carrots, peas, canned corn, broccoli, and tomato sauce
> - Wheat bread, bran muffins, saltines, graham crackers, granola bars, raisin bran, Fig Newtons, and oatmeal
> - Cranberry, apple, orange juice, maple syrup, low fat milk, and yogurt
> - Rice and baked potatoes
> - Baked beans, kidney beans, black beans, and lentils
> - Mac and cheese and pizza (yes, pizza!)

"Fiber keeps calories moving through your system faster," Kleiner advises. "Plus it makes you feel full."

So, avoid the fatty foods when possible, but rejoice in the idea that you can have as many carbs as proteins, if not more. (Caveat: again, I'm no nutritionist. Just a third baseman who can read.) We're all aware of the carbs out there. I could certainly spend the rest of my life eating bagels for breakfast, and then Coke and pizza the other five meals of the day. We should also be aware of the good eatin' protein foods. Quality sources of protein include beef, chicken breast, fish, and turkey, cheese, cottage cheese, eggs, milk, and yogurt, peanuts, and sunflower seeds (a staple for any good ballplayer), beans and lentils.

If I had a dollar for every time I picked up breakfast at Dunkin' Donuts or dinner at McDonald's, I'd have enough money to buy the entire team a round of Johnnie Walker Gold! Mickey D's is not what's being recommended here. But, if you can, eat a meal heavy in carbs before a game (an hour or two beforehand is optimal as this will give you plenty of fuel to burn). A bottle of Gatorade doesn't hurt, either. Gatorade provides carbs ripe for the burning, but also a ton of potassium that, among other benefits, can help to fight cramps. So, if not before first pitch then definitely as a part of your postgame routine, drink some sort of sports drink. Eat a banana or two, too. But if you fall prey to frequent charley horses, you might want to go a step further.

Dr. Michael Klaper, a nutritional specialist, writes, "Frequent leg cramps are often a sign of an electrolyte imbalance. I believe that part of the answer is to increase your intake of calcium and magnesium."

The good doctor recommends eating green, leafy vegetables like broccoli and kale for these vitamins. Another good source is calcium-fortified orange juice. Low-fat dairy products, sardines with bones (Yummy! Crunchy!!!), nuts, beans, and whole grains are also good.

Now let's say it's three in the morning and all of a sudden there's a fist squeezing your calf from the inside. For those of you who don't have some kale handy on the night table, get ready to massage. Flop out of bed without waking the wife, sit on the floor, and pull the cramped leg up to your chest, bending at the knee. Push your thumb gently into your calf, hold it there, and breathe normally until the cramp begins to relax. If this doesn't work, put your hands on either side of the cramp and roll the muscle from left to right. If this doesn't work, take two shots of tequila and call me in the morning.

Seriously, though, if this is a recurrent problem, direct intake of vitamins might be the preventive medicine your body needs. Vitamin E should be used to supplement daily dosages of up to 1,000 milligrams of magnesium and up to 1,000 milligrams of calcium.

On a different but related note, the vitamin and mineral supplement business has grown now to sales of more than $3 billion per year. And guess what? If you eat healthy and live an active life, most of these supplements are not necessary. When you eat decently, you get vitamins. That being said, adults, especially men, can use a daily dose of antioxidants. Vitamin C (citrus fruits, berries, and green leafy veggies), vitamin E (nuts and seeds), and beta-carotene (carrots, sweet potatoes, spinach, broccoli, and fruit)—all considered antioxidants—can reduce risk of cancer and heart disease. They also reduce the risk of tissue damage, which will keep you active and on the field of play.

And being active will help you avoid a case of the chubbies. The formula for identifying your ideal weight is even more simple than my drink-a-beer and divide-by-five equation. It's called the Body Mass Index, and the calculations are below:

$$\left(\frac{\text{Weight}}{\text{Height} \times \text{Height}} \right) \times 703 = \text{BMI}$$

A score of 18.5–24.9 = Normal
A score of 25–29.9 = Overweight
And a score of 30 and above = Obese
NOTE: *Use inches when calculating height.*

This formula, provided by the folks at the Center for Disease Control (CDC), taught me that I am a member of the Overweight Club and that if I'm not careful, I might never again have the chance to be careful, let alone crash the boards!

The CDC website states: "All persons who are obese or overweight should try not to gain additional weight . . . Whatever your BMI, talk to your doctor to see if you are at an increased risk for disease and if you should lose weight. Even a small weight loss (just 10% of your current weight) may help to lower the risk of disease."

Ten percent of 213 pounds is 21 pounds. Who're they kidding? Still, I appreciate that they're looking out for me. For us.

If you can burn 250 to 500 calories a day, every day, you can lose a pound per week. Walking and swimming are two great ways to burn calories without taxing your bad back or bum knees. Save that kind of self-inflicted damage for the season.

Everyone will tell you to form good habits at a young age. The problem is, at a young age, nobody wants to listen to anything old people have to say! By the time we see the wisdom of their ways, we're amongst them: aging, and fast.

Not only should you live an active life, you should live it enthusiastically. Doctors, nutritionists, advice columnists, and Misters French fries and Vickery all agree. Be actively engaged. Be passionate about the things you do. Don't let the years, let alone the ass kicking that is full-time employment, home ownership, and parenthood slow you down. Make sure to make time for yourself. And be passionate about the things you do. There's nothing wrong with an increased heart rate when the excitement is directed towards positive, productive activity. When you wake up in the morning, you ought to be able to hop out of bed with your heart racing in anticipation. There should be at least one thing that puts a smile on your face; something that even if you don't do it well, you do it with chutzpah.

I wholeheartedly embrace postgame poppers and beers chock-full of barley, hops, and empty calories. Living like that is great fun—it's part of what makes life so enjoyable. But we're only talking on occasion. The majority of meals should be handled a bit more carefully than those team happy hours. Be smart at home and at work and you can go out with the fellas, enjoying all of the deep-fried crap you want. In moderation, of course.

7

Weekend Warrior Hall of Fame: Bill Leete

Madison Beach and Rec has put their trust in Bill Leete for years now. Bill plays in the "A" League, but runs the "B" League and also the more relaxed "Fall Ball" League. He assigns the umps, decides whether or not to call games due to inclement weather, organizes the manager's meetings, and is responsible for turning off the lights when it's time for all of us beer-bellied bozos to get lost. Cut from the Grizzly Adams mold that is often associated with softball, Bill provides the kind of competent, calm leadership that every league needs. There are Hall of Famers like him all across the nation and they deserve some recognition every now and again.[18]

---

[18] *And Bill, if you're reading this, I am on Payne Environmental. That's capital "P," "a," "y," "n," "e." Payne!*

Without the Bill Leetes of the world, we weekend warriors would have nothing to do. We'd be like zombies in a George Romero flick: a bunch of lost souls wandering the streets with no games to play, no one to banter with, only *SportsCenter* and poker nights to satisfy our competitive needs. Thank you, Bill. You are a slayer of zombies and a facilitator of fun!

8

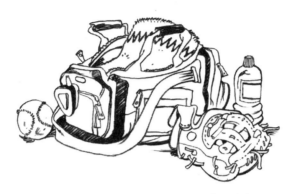

Earning a Call

I love the game because it's so simple, yet it can be so complex. There's a lot of layers to it, but they aren't hard to peel back.

—*Ernie Harwell*

OK, enough of this Richard Simmons crap. Let's play ball. More precisely, let's win.

If you're a rookie in the ranks of us weekend warriors or if you're just tired of losing and desperate for an angle, here it is: umpires can be swayed. Some of them can even be bought. That being said, I have never, ever cut a check for such a purpose.[19] And hopefully nobody in your league has, either. For the most part, umpires are blinder than Ray Charles and far less mobile. No, no, no, what I mean to say is . . . For the most part, umpires are upstanding guys just looking to hang around the ballpark and earn a couple of bucks. Just like yours and mine, their hearts swell with the sounds of the game. Either that or they're masochists whose one and only joy comes from ruining your Monday night. No, no, no, what I mean to say is . . . They'd be playing except that, for one reason or another, they just can't anymore. If you're stuck with idiots or blessed with the nation's fairest, what will work to your advantage is simply recognizing that umps are people, too.

Beware the Buzz!

Many a softball player has let his beer muscles get him into trouble. This is why I don't play "A" League in our town. Too much stupidity for me. Umpires will throw you out of the game and you can bet the mortgage they'll call the cops if you lay a hand on them. It is only a game. Don't let your barley brawn get the best of you. Save the Ron Artest imitation for Halloween.

---

[19] *Cash is harder to trace.*

Be cognizant of their feelings and you won't get kicked out. You may even earn a call later in the game.

Matt is a pro at this kind of thing. I believe it's 50 percent personality and 50 percent his positioning on the field. Over there at first, both the home plate umpire and the base umpire are well within earshot. Matt has interned at the Capitol, in Hartford, and his time with the politicians definitely didn't go to waste. He knows how to schmooze and he knows when to use words as weapons. Me, it's not my style. I root for my pitcher and when we're hitting, I'm the first one to pick a guy up after a sac fly. Barking at umps has never been my thing.

Here's a scenario for you, though. It's the second inning. On the back end of a double play, Matt stretches till the nail of his big toe is the only thing touching the bag. I mean, he looks like Nadia Comaneci during the floor exercises, doing a split to earn the gold, freedom from Communism, and hearts the world over. Well, OK, more like a youth league goalie stopping the puck from sliding through the five hole. We need this double play badly because the men of Payne are already down by a run and the other team's cleanup hitter is coming up. Matt's stretch seems to be enough to seal the deal as ball hits mitt, but the ump yells, "Tie goes to the runner!" Matt quickly scissors his legs closed, hops up into the air and then races to within three feet of the offending umpire; a respectable distance but also aggressive enough to send a message.

The lights in a big league stadium are too bright for shadows, but at town parks a man can cast four or five shadows. In this case, eight shadows meet to do battle on the infield dirt, the umpire's four shadows standing with the calm stoicism of a sumo; Matt's four attacking with the speed and intensity of a ninja.

He rants. He raves. He is expressive with his hands, turning back towards first and pointing out the fact that his foot stayed

Think with your head and your heart. Talk with your mouth and your hands. Win a call later in the game and perhaps an Academy Award the following winter.

on the bag and that the throw definitely, without a doubt, howcouldyoumissitBlue?, beat the runner. He does not curse, but he does carry on even after the ump has yelled, "Enough!" Only for another five seconds, though. Max. You see, Matt is smart enough to know that later on, the ump will give one back. If he's any good at all, there will be a makeup call. You can even see Matt smiling slyly as Tucker pushes him back towards first base. Just to make sure our point gets across, though, Joe, the loud-mouthed left fielder and de facto team captain, runs all the way in to reiterate Matt's points with Blue. Always refer to the ump as "Blue," by the way. Not "Blew" as in "you blew the call." Blue, as in the color of most umpire uniforms.

We all return to our spots, incensed over the call but hopeful for the future.

The cleanup hitter knocks the first pitch out of the park and now we're down by three. The inning ends in quiet disgrace, our forty shadows retreating lethargically from the field, but Payne

Environmental—a name that strikes fear in the hearts of men, women, and farm animals—isn't through yet. Not by a long shot. We chip away, eventually tying the score at 12–12. In the bottom of the seventh, Matt ignores the physics of time and the brace on his knee. He hauls ass as the shortstop double-clutches before throwing and surprise, surprise . . . Blue calls him safe! The other team argues halfheartedly, but everybody knows that this is just the way it goes.

A sacrifice fly bumps Matt to second and then Tucker's two-out single sends everybody's favorite supermodel sliding across home plate in a triumphant cloud of dust. Thirteen to twelve, Payne wins! Payne wins!! Payne wins!!!

After shaking hands with the other team, Matt takes the time to share his sentiment with the ump, "Good game, Blue. Good game." What a sport.[20]

Losing feels worse than winning feels good.

—Vin Scully

The second scenario is a little less dramatic: more schmooze and less singing of the blues. It's banter, real friendly-like and sure to garner at least one call during the season.

Make small talk. Ask questions. And make sure to act like you care about the answers. For example, find out which team the

---

[20] *Yes, that was a play on words. A double entendre, if you will.*

umpire follows. Is Blue a Yankee fan or a Red Sox fan? Mr. Met? Whatever you learn, catalog this information. Then, continue on your quest. Ask and observe. Observe and ask. Embrace your fellow man!

You know, now that I think about it, for some reason I've run across a lot of umps who are diabetic. (Perhaps this is why they're umpiring and no longer playing.) It doesn't hurt to ask the guy how he's feeling. Matt is also big on offering some of our water or Gatorade. And if you want to be a real artist about it, before kissing up, joke around with the obligatory: "Hey Blue, you take cash or checks?" You've now gotten the blatant brownnosing out of the way and it's time for the subtle stuff. Clearly, the offer of beverages or a leftover slice of pizza is just a nice gesture. No hidden agenda here . . .

This kind of thing pays off. It really does. Maybe not in that particular game, but a rec league only has so many umpires. Be nice to this guy and chances are you'll see him again over the course of the season. Think of it this way: with one well-placed question you've started to build capital. He remembers the uni, that ice-cold cup of Gatorade, the respectful young man who asked about the wife, kids, day job, impending hip surgery, and golf handicap. Come playoff time, favor may smile upon you. It *is* a game of inches . . .

Speaking of inches, this chapter cannot end without a word or two on ground rules. This year, everybody's favorite environmentalists got somewhat screwed when one of our guys hit a bomb that bounced into the woods and back out again. After touching home, Jon was called back for a ground-rule triple. We argued a bit, but let it go after a brief explanation. Then, in the seventh, the other team hit an identical ball and despite the raised hands of our outfielder (indicating the ball had gone into the woods before bouncing out again), their batter was allowed to round the bases and score. I stewed privately. Matt blew a gasket.

I feared for the safety of the umpire: it was a day game so he had no shadows to protect him. Matt is currently up the river, serving twenty-five to life. Some days you're just not going to come out on top . . .

Before every game, the umpires will ask each team to send a representative out for a review of the ground rules. We only play on two fields. Every game since I joined Payne Environmental has been on these two fields. At least eighty games, including fall ball, on these two fields. And still, the ground rules are discussed before every game. And still, Blue blows calls. Just make sure you know the rules and make a stink if you think you're right. Earn a call for later on or appeal to the home plate umpire and you just might get him to reverse the call. Save Blue from death at the hands of ninjas. Save your squad's version of Matt from sure conviction. Win the ball game.

Balls, Bats, Facts, and Stats:

On the topic of ground rules, fields with extremely short fences will often have a home run limit. It is important for a big hitter such as yourself to be aware of this limit (usually one, two, or three fence-clearing home runs allowed per team per game), lest you rip one and get charged with an automatic out.

9

Weekend Warrior Hall of Fame: Bill Plummer III

The more famous of the two Bills, Bill Plummer III is not only a member of the ASA Softball Hall of Fame, he is its curator, contact, and historian. This is a man who eats, breathes, and shi—sleeps softball!

Before taking on his current role at The Hall, Bill was its PR/media director. This is a perfect fit as he has written extensively about the sport, even contributing photographs to various publications. He has also been a manager and an umpire, but most gratifying of all, in 1996 he was the information manager when softball made its Olympic debut in Atlanta.

Bill, who hails from Syracuse, was inducted under the category of meritorious service in 1989. The ASA Hall of Fame, much like the Weekend Warrior Hall of Fame, is an exclusive group with limited membership. Despite the astounding number of people who play softball, Bill is one of less than three hundred inductees. The ASA Hall of Fame is located in Oklahoma City and is open to the public all year round.

NOTE:

Bill was also helpful in providing research for this book, so I'd like to thank him for that. He would've made my Hall even if he'd told me to go jump in a lake when I started asking questions, but as the icing on the cake he was a real swell guy; helpful as can be and an obviously huuuuge fan of the game. Thanks, Bill!

10

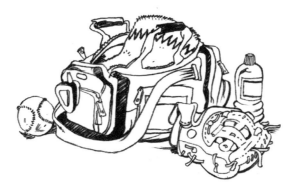

Talking the Talk
(Even If You Can't Quite
Walk the Walk)

No doubt, in these first few chapters you've picked up on my appreciation for the language of the game. It's banter like working the ump for a call. It's yelling "Move your ass or it's pine time!" to the guy who arrives at 6:29:59. It's informing the out-fielders how many outs there are and the catcher that you're coming home on a ground ball. It's whooping it up after a home run or hazing a teammate for taking a called third strike.[21] These are words and phrases that I love. They are the sounds of the game.

For the veterans out there, I know that this stuff is old hat for you. Just because I'm leaving no stone unturned doesn't mean

---

[21] *One team in Madison makes the guy not only bring all the beer, next game, he also has to wear a bright yellow shirt that says "WHIFFER" on the back . . .*

that I think you crawled out from under a rock. I know you weren't born yesterday—none of us weekend warriors were! Think of this as a primer for the rookies and a review for the rest. If you're not flipping through to learn the ropes, I suggest you let these words warm you on a cold winter night or revive you during a stint on the disabled list. Hear the banter echo off of the outfield bleachers, empty save the high school kids necking in the press box. Listen closely and you can hear yourself, embroiled in another nail-biter of a game . . .

As kids we learned how to talk the talk, even before we knew how to walk the walk. Eventually our skills measured up to our mouths, but now, those of us on the downside of our "careers" are relying, once again, on our verbal skills. Whether or not you can still deliver the goods on the field, the taste of the talk never does fade from the tongue. It's as synonymous with the game as the ping of ball on bat and the slap of ball in glove. Here are some of my favorite near-nonsensical, less-than-discreet softballisms:

BALL BANTER #1

1. "Hum now, come now!" I have no idea when or why I started saying this, but it's a cheer for the pitcher. Hum is a reference to really humming the ball in there. A fastball to make Nolan Ryan drool. I suppose it's not really relevant in slow-pitch softball, but old habits die hard. I had a lot of time on the bench in college to root for my fellow pitchers. And root I did. Hum one in there, man. Put 'im in the books! When Paul, Payne's steadfast hurler, slips one past the batter, chances are he was inspired by this call of the wild. Kind of.

    I guess I also have to touch on the second part of this particular phrase. "Hum now, *come now!*" OK, cover your virgin ears. (Earmuffs!) The "come now" is, indeed, a touch of sexual innuendo. It's a reference to the joy of firing a fastball past a guy. Admittedly, when a hitter strikes out in softball, it is more comical than orgasmic, but you get the point.

2. "Carter's a boy toucher!!!" This all-time favorite harkens back to my days with the Bleacher Creatures at Yankee Stadium. Clearly an attempt to get into the right fielder's head, I admit it's a little harsh for "B" league softball, but if your team needs a laugh, launch this sucker (especially if the opposing batter is a friend). "Mac's a boy toucher!" Say it loud, say it proud!!! Just try and save it for those 9:00 games when there are very few, if any, family members in the stands.

3. OK, enough of the nice stuff . . . Remember the subtleties of earning a call? Well, enough of that, too. Here's an indispensable gem for those hopeless, we're-about-to-get-mercy-ruled nights. Nights when it isn't the calls that are costing you the game but still, Blue isn't doing much to help. Yes indeed, it's, "Bend over and use your good eye, ump!" By the time Blue figures out what, exactly, you mean by "good eye" and why he'd have to bend over to see with it, the game will be looooong over. Hopefully.

Now that I've gotten that out of the way, here are some more commonly accepted terminologies. Feel free to use these without fear of physical harm or the risk of seeing your name in the police blotter.

BALL BANTER #2

1. "Ducks on the pond." Reserve this classic for when there are men in scoring position. This is one of my favorites, handed down from generation to generation of Howe men. What

hitter doesn't feel inspired when he hears "Ducks on the pond!"? It's second only to the *Rocky* theme song.[22]

2. "Pick me up" is a phrase the batter will fall back on if he falls prey to the infield fly rule. Or if he grounds out to the pitcher. Or if he (gulp!) strikes out. If there are runners on base and your teammate doesn't bring anyone home, doesn't even advance the runner, he'll ask you, the next batter, to pick him up. This means knocking in those ducks on the pond so that his failure can be glossed over. Go on, now. Pick your man up!

3. "Can o' corn." Back in the day, when grocery stores had shelves too high to reach, a bagger would knock the can off of the top shelf with a broom and there you'd be, camped out underneath the falling object of your desire (for convenience sake, let's say it is a can of corn . . .), gloveless but committed to bringing home dent-free vittles for the family. Not a problem since this was usually a relatively easy grab. Thus the phrase "can o' corn." Use it when one of your mates is tracking a lazy pop fly.

4. "Nice banana!" Used with a teammate, this is not just another sophomoric jeer of a cheer. It is a haze, however. Like a banana kick in soccer, if you need to lighten the mood after one of your fielders has thrown an unintentional curve ball, missing his target and getting charged with an error, you can refer to his throw as a "banana." And why not rub it in a little with the "nice?" Nice banana. Rolls right off the tongue. Plus, nothing gets 'em laughing like a little sexual innuendo.

5. A similar call, but intended for the other team, it's the ever-popular "Put a tent on that circus!!!" When they start dropping balls and/or throwing bananas all over the park, pull out this old standby. You'll be the toast of the town.

---

[22] *Officially titled "Gonna Fly Now" for all you trivia buffs.*

6. "The kangaroo court" returns us to intrasquad hazing . . . When a guy makes a mental error, a mistake of the mind if you will, he is threatened with the kangaroo court. Usually, if a major leaguer tosses the ball into the stands when there are still only two outs or if he misses the charter flight or if he runs through the third base coach's stop sign and is gunned out at home, he'll be charged a fine by the team's kangaroo court. The money goes into a charitable fund and a donation is made by the team at the end of the season. In slow-pitch softball, the team is everyone's favorite charity and the bonehead in question usually has his feet held to the fire at the bar. In the least, he brings the food and/or drink to the next game. Screw up physically and you will find only empathy of the most familiar kind. Have a brain fart, however, and the kangaroo court will get you.

7. Speaking of beer, if you care to haze another player's hat, feel free. One of my favorite put-downs is the "six-pack hat." The specific usage is up to you, but what this refers to is the flat brim of a brand new lid. If a guy is foolish enough to show up without breaking in his hat, with a crown as high as a John Deere and a brim not yet curled to near-horseshoe proportions, have at him. If his brim is so straight that you can balance a six-pack on it, he deserves to get the business from you!

8. Know enough to "throw it around the horn" if you're an infielder. Please. This is basic baseball knowledge and it definitely extends to softball (unless you're on a field that has no lights and it is quickly approaching dusk. Then, it's a faux pas to throw the ball around the horn after an out.) A ground ball out should go from first to short to second to third and back to the pitcher. That being said, by request all of our around-the-horn horniness ends with Matt over there at first.

Most teams finish with the throw to third, but Matt likes to be a part of the fun. There is certainly room for improvisation here, just don't be the bonehead who starts throwing it around when there's a runner on base. That's the kind of thing that gets you fined by the kangaroo court.

9. "Nice sac!" Again, not everything has to be bathroom humor or a celebration of the male genitalia. Just half of everything. But in this case, at least, "sac" is merely an abbreviation of "sacrifice." Pick a guy up when he hits a long fly that scores a run. Show him how much you care by commenting on his philanthropic sac.

10. "Bad hose" or "bad wing." Use these terms when asking someone if they have a sore arm. If the answer is yes, let him play catcher or second base. The other team will undoubtedly capitalize on his bad hose, otherwise . . .

11. In a different vein, spread the word if you notice that an opposing outfielder has a "rag arm" or "squirt gun." This is a guy you can run on all day . . .

12. If an opposing player bowls over your catcher and your catcher is the team patriarch, a sixty-year-old grandfather-type who only comes out for one game a year and who didn't even have the ball in his glove, "That's bush." Bush is a dig at the forty-third president. No it isn't. Politics has no place on the field of play. What I meant to say is, bush is short for "bush league," a reference to a level of baseball that is even lower than the minor leagues, even lower than D-III JV. "That's bush" can be used to describe a variety of acts, most of which are intentional and cheap. When it comes to retaliation, keep in mind that even though you're not wearing metal spikes, you can still slide cleats high.[23]

---

[23] *My favorite retaliation, however, comes with a nod to the scoreboard at the end of the game.*

13. A "rubber game" is the deciding game in a series. Any time you are playing the final game in a series that is tied, you are playing a rubber game. And no, this has nothing to do with safe sex or galoshes.

14. "That's a dying quail . . . " A good thing if your teammate hit it, a bad thing if not. A dying quail is a blooper that lands right between the infield and the outfield for a single. Just watch out for the Charlie Hustle types who stretch these into doubles so as to get into scoring position and save some face. "Knubber," "flare," and "dink" are other ways of referring to these seeing-eye hits.[24] And if your teammate gets on base this way, somebody is sure to yell, "It'll look like a line drive in the box score tomorrow." Oh blessed banter. Sure sounds better on base than on the bench!

15. The opposite: a "smash," "blast," "jack," or "hot shot." You can say that the ball was "laced," "launched," "peppered," "ripped," "pounded," "scorched," "smacked," or "stroked" when somebody gets a hold of one. And feel free to celebrate a home run by calling it a "dinger," "big fly," "bomb," "moon shot," "rainmaker," or "tater." When somebody on your squad "goes yard," you might as well get loud about it. Live vicariously!

---

[24] *Dying quails and opposite-field pokes do not make for the most macho of at-bats, but all of the best softball hitters are more likely to try for one of these than going for the fences. They know better, hint, hint . . .*

Beware the Buzz!

If you are single and on the prowl, don't rely too much on this kind of ball banter when chatting up a young lady after the game. If you're lucky, you may get away with one "nice sac" joke, but don't push it. Not many women are impressed with softball stories, let alone softball humor.

11

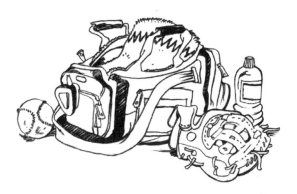

Weekend Warrior Hall of Fame: Mr. Rotisserie Baseball . . . Daniel Okrent

It was while in transit, in November of 1979, that Daniel Okrent first made his bid to be one of the greatest men in history. Like, better than Benjamin Franklin even.

On his way to Austin, Texas, Okrent was excited to eat at his favorite barbecue joint, The Pit. Thus the name for his fantasy: The Pit League. But his friends in The Lone Star State—more concerned with cattle futures than future stars—thought that he was being a dork, so it wasn't until Okrent's New York friends agreed to play that the first fantasy baseball league was formed. Their initial discussion was held at a French restaurant named (you guessed it) La Rotisserie Francaise. Rotisserie baseball was born.

Okrent and his fellow authors and editors officially formed the league in January of 1980 and twenty-five years later, many a weekend warrior is able to make good use of his time in the office, checking stats and standings before the day's first cup of coffee has been finished!

I mentioned before that if you're reading this book, it might be the off-season. Well, one benefit to playing fantasy baseball is the hot stove league. You've never followed off-season trades and resignings until you've managed a team of your own. My spirits in the dark days of winter go where The Flying Eskimos go . . .

12

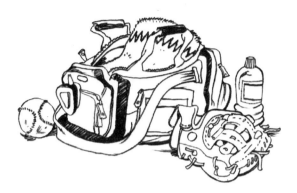

You Got Gear

Do not play in pants.
End of story.

OK, I'll explain further. My advice to you is to buy loose-
fitting athletic shorts and not those overpriced, 99 percent
polyester, caulk-colored softball pants. And get your shorts
cheap: two or three pairs at Wal-Mart or Kohl's or wherever.
Once you have them, plan on shredding them in fits of athletic
ecstasy: sliding into second just ahead of the throw, diving for a
line drive, wrestling Bubba, your 130-pound catcher, to the
ground after winning the championship. You get the picture.

If you're already a wearer of softball pants, I don't mean to
offend. And I know, a lot of players do wear them. It's just that
they're so damned hot. And the first time you slide you're not

only going to rip them, you're sure to cut up your leg same as wearing shorts. I will say this, though: if the other fifteen players on the team are sporting them, obviously you should do the same. But unless it's a team trend or a league rule, my advice is to go with the shorts.

I just know that I sweat when I play. I could be standing like a statue at third base and still I'd be sweating. Standing still, though, is something I do not do. I don't want to get a shot off of the face (or worse), so I stay super aware throughout the game. Plus, I get emotionally involved. The heart is pumping and the feet are never idle because, you know, idle feet are the devil's work. (Wasn't that a Benjamin Franklin maxim, too?) I'm keeping the legs warm with quick stretches, I'm talkin' Yankee baseball with Tucker at shortstop, I'm waving to my wife and daughter, I'm trying to peg the third-base coach in the cleat with a pebble, I'm adjusting my cup and wiping sweat from my brow. Thus, the perspiration. If I were to wear softball pants, my crotch would become a virtual oven. How can I be expected to concentrate on ground balls when my butt cheeks are doing their best imitation of Niagara Falls?! Granted, pants do provide a slight buffer when you dive or slide, but I have a remedy for that.

There are two things you'll need to get so as to avoid all manner of open wounds and gangrene. One is sliding pants. These are really just glorified spandex, shorts that feature padding in all the right places. The other thing you'll want to pick up, even before sliding your way into that first glorious gash (I wear my scabs as a badge of honor and I know you do, too!), is some sort of protective pad. Mizuno makes the one that I wear on my sliding leg.[25] They call it a "sliding knee pad," but I land hard on the area just

---

[25] *The pop-up slide is a thing of sheer beauty. Right leg straight, left leg curled underneath . . . Right heel catches bag and I'm standing in a cloud of dust. "Safe!"*

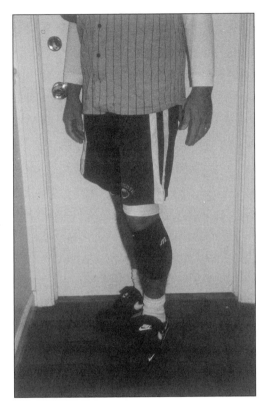

Here is how I protect against those boy-I-wish-I-hadn't-slid raspberries. Because never, ever should you not slide just to save some skin!

below my knee and to the left of my shin, so that's where I wear it. Before buying it (approximately $9), I could actually trace what momentum and a few thousand grains of infield dirt had done to my skin. This sliding pad is six or seven inches long and made of a stretchy combination of spandex, polyester, and cotton with a neoprene pad. After sliding, it takes me all of three seconds to roll it down, brush out the dirt, and get back to business, raspberry-free.

So, go with shorts, the sliding pants, and one of these sliding pads and you should be just fine. Slide feet-first, by the way. To my knowledge, Mizuno doesn't make neoprene nipple pads.

Now, let's take it from the top. Or, rather, the bottom. Feet first.

This is rec league softball. Nobody is going to let you wear metal spikes. So, if you played college ball, it's finally time to toss 'em out. Make sure, though, to get yourself a new pair of cleats. Don't just say to yourself, "Ah, it's only softball. I'll wear my sneakers." No, no, no, my friend. If you respect your groin, you *will* wear cleats. Running back and forth on grass is tremendously taxing on the nether regions. In the least, you are guaranteed to have a hard time walking the next day. Remember Alice after the *Brady Bunch* rode mules down into the Grand Canyon? She had one mighty big hitch in her gitch after dismounting. Don't get caught looking like Alice. It's no way to enter a meeting and it's no way for your children to see you. And besides, they don't care: they'll still want to be chased. Shredded groin or no shredded groin.

So, spend the $40. Regular, run-of-the-mill cleats will do—just something to help you get a grip. And like the anti-raspberry body armor, you'll want to pick up your new go-fasters *before* the season begins. Traction is especially important in the early season when spring showers are still making the ground treacherous. Also, if you have a 9:00 game, you'll find that dew settles early. It's hard enough to throw a guy out at home with a wet ball. Make sure that you can actually keep your feet and get to the ball.

Another good argument for buying cleats is that, at our age, speed is fleeting. When trying to advance the runner, you squib a grounder to second, you'll want to get out of the batter's box and beat it on down the line as quickly as possible. Never, ever get doubled up in softball. Never. It's embarrassing, man. Deceased ancestors will roll over as you soil the family name and the live ones will want to disown you. Even with cleats you might not get there in time, but they're your only hope. Avoid familial shame. Run like hell.

In the effort to leave no stone unturned, let me add this advice to the mix. Under those cleats . . . socks. Absorbent athletic socks. I know you don't really need me to tell you to wear socks, but I'm doing it anyway. I sometimes go sockless in golf and the only time I regret it is coming out of a sand trap. The entire infield is like a sand trap, folks. Thus, you'll never find this bat head sans socks. I wear regular ol' socks in the regular ol' style, but I've seen a lot of guys pull their hose (thin baseball socks) up all the way. I think this may be their remedy for the dreaded raspberries and subsequent gangrene.

Before continuing with this interesting sock talk, let's take a minute to contemplate all that belongs in your bag. Here's what I carry in my college knapsack (aka equipment bag):

THE OL' EQUIPMENT BAG

1. Standard-issue Louisville Slugger glove (I lost my baseball glove, but had a softball party and somebody who partied a bit too much forgot his glove and never called to reclaim it. Know when to say when . . .).
2. Batting glove.
3. The much-discussed sliding pad.
4. Water bottle.
5. Cell phone, so as to never be out of touch with the folks at home. I do whatever I can to keep everyone happy (and my name on the roster and off of that shit list!).
6. Wallet. Full, preferably.
7. Advil for the back. I give out as many as I take; this is all a part of being a good teammate.
8. League schedule (helpful because half the time even the umps don't know who's supposed to be the home team).
9. An extra ball or two for the quick warm-up.
10. Cup (jock's already on.)
11. Cleats.
12. A pen (because I think it's been there since college).

Now, back to the footwear. I do have one last piece of legitimate sock advice to share: remember to pull them *out* of your equipment bag AFTER EVERY GAME!!! I drive back and forth in flip-flops and my bag is big enough to hold everything listed above and naturally, I stuff those nasty socks into the bag with the cleats after the game. If I do this on a Wednesday night and we don't play again till the following Monday . . . things can start to smell a bit gamy in there. Ever smell a hockey player's bag? Yeah, like that. Cat piss meets year-old cheese.

Last season, I did the "stuff and forget" three games in a row and found myself sockless upon arrival. This meant pulling two socks from the bottom of the bag, shaking the moisture and dirt out of them, and then rolling them back onto my feet. Like eating regurgitated worm and that, my friends, is for the birds!

Trust me, empty the bag when you get home.

Beware the Buzz!

Let the nasty sock syndrome be your incentive to stop drinking after the second or third postgame beer. I find if I have the fourth, it's all I can do to crawl into bed when I get home. On these nights, the least of my problems is the sock-and-jock compost pile in my bag. It's the earful I get in the morning after my wife realizes that I didn't shower when I got home and that now, half of the infield is in bed with her. (Meaning the dirt, not Tucker, Jonny Sic, and Matt!)

Just north of that sliding pad is four layers of fun. Or three, if you count my cup and jock ensemble as one and the same. On top of my man girdle are the sliding shorts and then the athletic shorts. If I go out after the game, most of the time I take the time to remove the jock in the bathroom of the bar. I just can't hang out when feeling so—how shall I say it?—encumbered. Speaking of which, I wear a T-shirt under my jersey. In the car, a spare T-shirt for stepping out afterwards.

Dear Abbey: Why can't I just wear the sweaty T-shirt, using it as a napkin as I inhale my wings? ~Metrosexual in Madison

These are my problems, not yours, so that's the last of that. Party in your jock, if you like. Wear that one lucky T-shirt all year long. To each weekend warrior his own!

Speaking of luck and superstition, I only have a couple of hats deemed appropriate for game wear. For some reason, one is a golf hat. I think I like that it's orange. (Maybe I am a metrosexual . . . Pedicure, anyone?) More likely than not, though, it had something to do with a good game way back when. Once a month I run it through the dishwasher and the smell becomes bearable again.[26]

The second hat is more appropriate. It's the Yankee hat that I absconded from the wife a few years back. It just fit so nicely . . . And after three or four wearings, the combination of sun and sweat had really broken the fibers down into the shape of *mi cabeza*. She sniffed it once and said it was mine. I took that as a sign of good fortune and so here we are.

This hat is also on the monthly dishwasher plan. I obviously alternate washings, so that I never have to go without. God forbid I need to wear a different lid. That'd be like stepping on the foul lines or congratulating the pitcher on his no-hitter after the third inning.

---

[26] *I do this more for family, friends, and teammates than for myself.*

On a related note, I switch the hat I wear when playing a series against a team called Nick's Place (good burgers and even better softball players). Their pitcher is crafty. He's got a great memory, which is an essential for any and all pitchers. This guy can get me to fly out to deep left. Every time. So, I will switch my hat and my stance a little, hoping to *not* jog his memory. Desperate times call for desperate measures.

There is a third hat, but I only bust that out for "A" League games. As compensation for not making the "B" League championship move up to the "A" League, each "B" League team has to play against the big boys three times during the season. When we take these guys on—fellas who eat barbed wire because they have it tattooed on their biceps—I pull out the old Hobart hat. You know, for good luck. After all, I was a winning pitcher, the all-time winningest at the D-III JV level. Cooperstown, here I come!

Truth be told, the hat brings me as much luck now as it did back then, which is not much. (We were 0-3 against the "A" Leaguers this year.) Until my hat learns how to nab those speed-of-light one-hoppers down the line, I doubt it's going to do me or the men of Payne any good. Still, superstition is superstition. You've got to trust your gut instinct, especially when your gut is as prolific as mine.

Before moving on, I'll say that I don't bother with sunglasses or eye black, but really that's because it isn't necessary on the fields where I play. The sun field is out in right, so I never have to contend with it. I once played in a one-pitch fall ball league. The field was gorgeous, tucked under the Tappan Zee Bridge and right next to the Hudson River, New York's skyline shimmering to the left, and the sun setting over The Palisades. Unfortunately, from third base, I could only see the silhouette of the three wise men—umpire, catcher, and batter—because that sun was right behind home plate. In that case, I did wear eye black and it helped.

The important thing to note about that story, though, is not the eye black but the idea of a one-pitch league. The batter comes up with a 3–2 count and either walks, strikes out, or puts the ball in play. The games fly by, usually lasting no more than forty-five minutes. It really is a workout, on par with fast-pitch softball (if not more so). You are constantly running on and off the field, around the bases, after bloop singles and line drives, back into the dugout, back onto the field, with not a moment to rest. And God forbid you have to score from first and then take the field two pitches later. "Oxygen!!!"

But as far as what to wear, I think it comes down to a combination of personal preference and what the other guys are doing. With the Internet, you'll be able to find just about anything you could ever want or need. Around here we've got Mo's and Dick's and Bob's and any number of places that will be glad to fill an order for you. But I find the best prices are generally online. You can feel free to shop without worry of being pegged a metrosexual!

Balls, Bats, Facts, and Stats:

One of the keys to having fun in softball is not wasting your money. And the number-one waste of cash for softball-playing weekend warriors is . . . (drum roll, please) . . . the illegal softball bat. Go to *http://www.softball.net/bats.html* for the latest on legal and illegal bats.

13

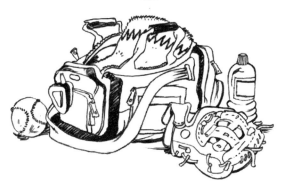

Weekend Warrior Hall of Fame: The Hooters Championship Series

In recent years, the Hooters restaurant chain has shown its love of sport by becoming involved in auto racing, golf, and swimsuit competitions. In 2001, they even decided to collaborate with the ASA as lead sponsor of their slow-pitch championship tournament. Between that and the buffalo wings, not to mention their dress code, how could I not induct Hooters into the Weekend Warrior Hall of Fame?

Plus, it's fun to say "Hooters!"

The setup is this: local tournaments produce winners who advance to the national tournaments held over Labor Day weekend. The winning teams from the East and West National Championship Finals get to participate in the Hooters-USA Slow-Pitch Championship, held every October at the ASA Hall of Fame Complex in Oklahoma City. It is a three-out-of-five, winner-take-all, balls-to-the-walls series!!!

Easton supplies the equipment, Miller Lite supplies the beer, and an unspecified airline (Hooters Air, perhaps?) provides fifteen roundtrip tickets to each team. There are also complimentary hotel rooms for all. Thank you, Hooters![27]

---

[27] *A press release from back when the agreement was reached states, "As part of the sponsorship agreement, Hooters of America will also provide on-site hospitality provided by the 'nearly world famous' Hooters Girls." Nice.*

14

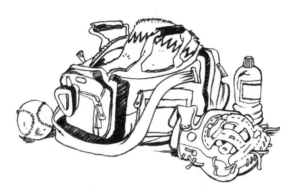

Why Softball is Actually Better Than Baseball

I like playin' softball, but watchin' baseball? I don't want to knock the national pastime, but mister, a lot of nothin' happens.

—*Elvis*

Why is softball better than baseball? Well, in simplest terms: the ball is bigger and the field is smaller.

In a perfect world, I would play baseball till I was ninety. I could go off for a day of play and not miss half of my daughter's life. But I've played hardball before. It takes all day. I love the game, but I don't have that much time. The best I can manage is six hours for golf and six hours means you're just finishing the sixth inning in the first game of a doubleheader.

Besides, it'd cost me too much to buy a plane ticket if I wanted to go from first to third on a single. I mentioned that the field is smaller in softball, didn't I? It makes a tremendous difference. If you don't believe me, take a drive to the local high school and try running the bases. You'll need oxygen by second base, a defibrillator by the time you reach home.

Yes, it's true. You don't have to run or throw quite as far in softball and yet a double play is still a close play!

The last at-bat I had for the Newburgh Expos was against a lefty and he struck me out. Looking. This guy dropped down for a little sidearm action and quick-as-can-be the pitch zoomed towards my belly button. Instinctively, I opened up the front foot, threw my butt back towards the third base coach, and then watched in disbelief as the ball slid ever so gently back over the inside black of the plate. Shit like that doesn't happen in softball. I can guarantee you that.

Another reason? In baseball, you have to wear pants. And you know how I feel about the *pantalones.*

Metal spikes are allowed and getting spiked really, really hurts. I don't miss getting spiked. That would be like wanting to relive the night I asked my in-laws for Alicia's hand in marriage. It took me four hours, her parents and sister stringing me along because they knew what was coming. And well, it sucked. But at least they said yes. There's nothing good about getting spiked: no happy hugs after the deed is done. Getting spiked is like a nasty divorce . . . with kids involved.

Another reason why softball is better than baseball: the cheerleaders.[28]

Actually, hit batters is what I mean to say. Right up there with getting spiked is taking a fastball in the back. And I'm not even including the prospects of a bench-clearing brawl. Now granted, there can be fights in softball, but when hit in the head with a high arcing pitch, it just doesn't carry quite the same weight. By eliminating the head hunting and back bruises, that right there is proof enough for me. Like Elvis, softball is king.

I almost forgot, another reason is that old guys just don't look good in a baseball uniform. It comes back to the pants. And a tucked-in jersey. Not so flattering when the stomach isn't flat. Let's leave the unis to the young studs. We need our jerseys untucked, the material hanging so low in front and even lower in back, so as to cover our country-sized derrieres.

There are plenty of good, appropriate sports for us aging weekend warriors. Criteria for the following list included things like having energy enough to party afterwards and, even more importantly, maintaining dignity.

---

[28] *Just checking to see who's paying attention. Carry on, good reader. Carry on.*

TOP FIVE SPORTS FOR
AGING WEEKEND WARRIORS

5. Bowling

4. Football (touch football, of course; don't be an idiot)

3. Golf

2. Basketball (plenty of opportunity to embarrass yourself, but the health benefits make the risk well worth it)

1. Softball (we are soft and so is the sport, if not the ball)

And if you're still not convinced of the merits of softball over baseball, I have one last card to play; my ace in the hole. Have you ever seen a keg on the field during a baseball game? I didn't think so . . .

I'd walk through hell in a gasoline suit to keep playing baseball.

—*Pete Rose*

15

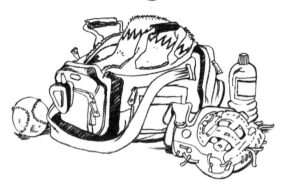

You've Got Game Now, But No Idea Where to Play It

If you're a weak-hitting middle infielder, there's always a team looking for a good glove.

If you're a red-meat-eatin' crusher of spheres, there's always a team in need of your bat.

If you're a beer-drinking bench warmer, there's always a bench with your name on it. And these days, they're made of aluminum, so no need to pull splinters out of your butt after the game!

If you're a fleet-footed former Legion star, well past your prime but still speedy enough for one or two triples per game, there's always a team looking for a new leadoff hitter. Pronto.

If you don't mind shelling out $50 for the umpires and the jersey, there are always teams more than willing to cash your check.

Before I beat this dead horse into glue, here's the deal: if you're looking for a game, the country is chock-full of leagues.

Anyone who's ever opened childproof aspirin or filed a tax return is resourceful enough to find a spot on a roster. Maybe the issue is finding a league or maybe it's just a matter of finding the *right* league, I don't know. But I'll speak to both.

Softball spans a spectrum. On the one hand, you have leagues geared towards last decade's Jennie Finches and Lisa Fernandezes; towards modern day Ty Stofflets and Eddie Feigners. On the other hand, there is slow-pitch, just perfect for folks looking to hang out and have fun. But like they say about the lottery, you gotta be in it to win it. Or to lose it. Or to tie it. Or to play three innings in the rain just to have the game called and then you and some other knuckleheads slide your way around the basepaths in a fit of soggy joy not seen, heard, sniffed, or felt since the days of field trips and recess.

Just be in it!

Wait for an invitation and you're just another couch potato. I have made frequent references to inactivity and nutritional neglect. Far worse in many ways are the folks who commit every week's *TV Guide* to memory. I'm telling you, couch-as-coffin just ain't the way to live, brother.

When I was seven, we buried Grandpa Tenace with a poster of Wonder Woman. An eighty-five-year-old immigrant from Italy and he went to his grave with the ever-buxom, blue-eyed Linda Carter by his side. Grandpa Tenace never set foot on a softball field—bocce, perhaps, as a young man, sambuca in hand—but I will hold him up as an example, nonetheless. He loved Wonder Woman, but was no TV junkie. He had his tomato garden and he loved to walk the neighborhood. Once a week, he'd settle in for his favorite show, but other than that, no boob tube. The irony is, if he'd been a lazy couch potato of a boob-tube watcher, he never would have lived long enough to watch *Wonder Woman*. He would have departed this world in his sixties or seventies, never having set eyes upon his true love. Behold the rewards of a long-lived life!

It's out there, waiting for you to start living it again. Sure, those training to run a marathon or climb Mt. Everest might look down upon the sports we weekend warriors play, but that's fine by me. I'm not looking to conquer any heights and I'm not looking to impress any real athletes. I gave that gig up back when I was twenty. All I'm looking to do is shake off the rust a couple of times a week. If you don't get out there and start shaking, your family is going to come down one morning and find the Tin Man frozen stiff on the couch. Life: the best reality show there is.

OK, I'm done with the preaching. It's time, once more, for the teaching.

I lucked into my softball league. The fact that its speed and intensity (or lack thereof) suits me is just icing on the cake. I had just finished a two-year stint recovering from a herniated disc that nearly sent me to surgery. Herniate a disc so badly that your high tops grow moss, your glove gets moldy, and your golf clubs are only good for hosting Charlotte's web and you get an extra appreciation for pickup games and rec leagues, municipal courses and flag football. To be able to walk onto the softball field again was such a huge relief that the level of competition didn't even matter.

I can't imagine if I hadn't made that call . . .

When we moved to town, my wife joined the Newcomers Club. I thought it was a little hokey, but I also know that when my fantasy baseball team won it all two years ago—my finest athletic feat in nearly a decade—she didn't look at me in quite the same way Melinda looks at Bill Gates. My victories were becoming more and more minor as my waistline grew more and more prominent. Anyway, I went with her to a Christmas party and met her friend's husband. Jon was nice enough, but men generally don't ask favors of other men, especially when they've just met . . . under the mistletoe! But two months later, with spring right around the corner, I got the urge. The better half had made a passing reference to Jon playing a lot of sports. It stuck in the back of my head like a thorn in the lion's paw. With no mouse in sight, I pulled that thorn out myself. I got the phone number from Alicia, swallowed all male instinct (there is nothing in the masculine makeup that permits chatting in any way, shape, or form), and asked him if there might be a spot on the team.

He couldn't have been nicer. (He even took the photo below, so that I could be in it. That Jon is a righteous dude!) Payne was already three weeks into their season, but a few of the guys had proven themselves to be unreliable, so I was welcomed aboard. The thorn was gone, my pride was intact, and the mold was wiped from my glove with vigor. I covered the thing with shaving cream, loosened it up, and got down to the field as fast as I could, nearly hyperventilating as I ran out to shag flies!!!

Good times with good men (even if they don't necessarily smell so good!). The author is the guy in the hat.

Make a call of your own if you're looking for a league. There might not be an immediate connection, but there's always a community bulletin board at the grocery store or town rec department. Oftentimes, leagues in need will advertise in the local newspaper. And if you see some guy in a uniform, buying mineral ice and/or Advil and/or a heating pad at the drug store, don't be afraid to ask. Women are good about this when it comes to baby talk. They see that stroller and they stroll right over. Next thing they know, they've learned about everything from local lactation consultants to the top day care centers. Do the same. You probably won't gain any insight into breast-feeding, but you might just find yourself a team in transition, a team that needs you!

16

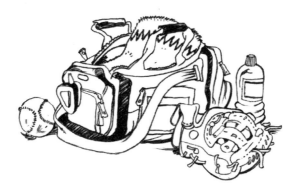

Charity Begins at Home (Plate)

There is a crossroads in western New York where winds from the north country collide with the precipitation of the Great Lakes. It was here, twenty miles from the southern shores of Lake Ontario, that I went to college. It was here that I first played snowball.

The cold weather months don't offer up too many social options in Geneva. There's drinking in front of the television. Or you could go out to a bar and drink. You could sneak your drinks into the movie theater or you could get physical for an hour or two and go bowling. And drink. But if you don't want to drink and if, by chance, you don't want to study, there just isn't much to do. But one February we were given an option. For a good cause, too.

Tom, a fraternity brother with a penchant for Pabst Blue Ribbon and the Washington Redskins, had read of this event in the paper and shared the news.

"Softball? In the snow? Are you serious?!"

Once we got over the oddity, momentum built like when Belushi rallies his boys to create the Delta "Deathmobile" for the homecoming parade. This wasn't just a good idea. It was a *fantastic* idea. Still . . .

"First game is 8:00?" someone asked. "In the morning?"

"Yep. We leave for the field at 7:30. Sharp!"

And then the banter began in earnest. Tom had his team.

So it was that on a cold and snowy Saturday morning in February of 1992, I pulled on two sets of long underwear, several layers of T-shirts and sweats, snow pants and freshly waterproofed work boots, a bright orange hunting hat, and two batting gloves. There would be no remote controls this day. It was time to play.

Lake-effect snow can leave western New York buried from October to April. But on that field—McCoy Stadium, home of the Geneva Cubs of the New York–Penn League—it was like ten flowers sprouting through the crust of snow whenever a team took the field. We could practically feel spring blowing its gentle winds when the thermometer broke twenty degrees sometime after high noon. The bat twanged like a tuning fork when contact was made, but nobody cared. This was better than bowling or cow tipping, hands down!

We were now a part of a tradition, and better yet, a charitable tradition. Every February for I don't know how many years, the Geneva Lion's Club has hosted this tournament as a fun fundraiser. Simple as pie from the Red Jacket Orchard, we paid our entrance fee and next thing you know, we were trying to beat out base hits in drifts measuring half-a-foot. The opposing catcher thought that throwing a hidden snowball back to his pitcher was the funniest thing he'd ever seen and how could we not agree? Laughing raises the body temperature, so laugh we did! Sliding does too, so we slid. And we dove. And we made snow angels. The infielders played everything like a bunt and the outfielders were no more than twenty feet behind the infield dirt. Wherever that was! Balls may fly out of Coors Field, but in February nothing flies far unless you're in Florida. Geneva, New York is no Florida.

Aside from the obvious fun, this was a great way to bring people together. Townies never like the college kids much, but there we were, toe-to-toe in the snow. The teams from town learned that not all of Hobart's students are spoiled brats. Not so intellectual, either. (Intellectual frat boys is an oxymoron anyway, isn't it?) You've got to be downright idiotic to play softball in twenty-degree weather, right?! Either that or you like to stop and smell the roses. No matter how frozen they may be.

In California, there is the annual March of Dimes Sno-Ball, a fundraising event that has been played for more than twenty years now. The tournament, held in North Tahoe, usually draws close to one hundred teams. There are a number of divisions, including fast and slow-pitch as well as men, women, and co-ed. A well-organized affair, for sure. Closer to my home, the Connecticut Bar Association holds a winter softball event to benefit homeless shelters for women and children in New Haven. Ten years old now, this snowball tournament is part of a month-long fundraising effort. For twenty years, Louisville, Kentucky, has also played host to a January event: a single elimination tournament for charity. In the past, the March of Dimes has been the beneficiary. The last two years, the $100 team entry fee has gone to the Kentucky Recreation and Park Society Scholarship Fund. I love it. I love the idea of fun with a purpose. I love the idea that fraternity boys aren't the only ones crazy enough to don work boots and batting gloves!

As I remember it, we were swept that day and were back at Delta Chi by 2:00, thankful to get out of the cold. Two games was enough fun for us. Glory days don't have to be all about winning.

17

A Return to Couchdom

I'm feeling guilty about the couch-as-coffin comment. Not necessarily hypocritical, but a bit too judgmental. After all, I like ass-sitting just as much as the next guy.

Even weekend warriors need to kick up their heels every now and again, regain control of the remote control and log an hour or three on the couch. So, here it is, my friends, a return to our kingdom—a return to couchdom.

When it comes to bats and balls, there are plenty of opportunities for plopping down and being a spectator. I will admit, my favorites all involve hardball, but I can recommend at least one softball event for your viewing pleasure.

In late spring, right about the time most kids return home for summer, some of them stay behind to play in the NCAA Tournament: young women with even less time than major league baseball players to decide whether to swing or take the pitch; women manning (pun intended) the hot corner with less time than Graig Nettles to react to hot shots; women in visors, running for home with a trophy in mind.

And anyone who thinks this couldn't possibly be fun to watch has never seen Jennie Finch pitch her Arizona Wildcats to a championship. As a bonus, she's kind of hot—meaning the movement she gets on her pitches. Unhittable!

Now, if this hasn't captured your interest, if you're thinking I haven't a thing to say about anything related to *watching* sports, hang in there. Not only do I have something to say on the matter, I also have a recipe to share. Yes, a recipe. You know, for cooking. I'm like the Martha Stewart of softball, but with less makeup and more flatulence. I think . . .

But before the chili recipe, I've got to brag a little about something I witnessed, firsthand. Actually, two somethings. When it comes to your viewing pleasure, friends, you just can't beat the American League Championship Series. In football, the conference championship games are usually better than the Super Bowl, and the same is true in baseball. Especially if the series involves the Red Sox and Yankees.

The last two years, I've been able to watch these two teams meet up in the deciding game 7. That's right, not once but twice, with the chance to go to the World Series on the line. And not from my couch, either. I've been there—no corporate connection, no business box, no suit and tie special; Ticketmaster tickets, fees, taxes, naming rights to my firstborn, and all!!—in the flesh, in The House That Ruth Built. The House That Schilling Burnt Down.

As a Yankee fan, I've felt the highest of heights and the lowest of lows. When Aaron Boone hit that dinger off of Tim Wakefield, I screamed myself hoarse, the better half crying with joy by my side, and 56,000 of my best friends partying like it was 1999. But it wasn't 1999 last year. It wasn't even 2003. It was a new dawn for Red Sox Nation and I was there for that Beatdown in the Bronx. Great theater, but man was it tough to see. And for those of you who can't see it in person, treat the baseball postseason as a spectacle to be enjoyed from the comfortable confines of your own home. Put the kiddies to bed and drink coffee. You'll have to make it past midnight to see the dramatic home runs, the walk-off base knocks, the corn-fed closer striking out the side, but it's worth it. Even subjecting yourself to those mindless Fox promos is well worth it. And if you follow my recipe, you can show your disapproval of such shows, and their stars sitting in prime box seats, by farting. Yes, I will help you to reach new heights of dignity, friends. After all, it is your right as an American to send a floating air biscuit towards your television set!

Be patient, young chef. The recipe is coming . . .

While I'm at it, the All-Star Game ain't a half bad show, either. I don't like the new home-field advantage thing, but at least our guys are playing defense. The NBA and NFL games are a joke, but in baseball, the pitchers really pitch and the hitters really hit. I know I argued that softball is better than baseball, but that's for when old guys are playing. When given the opportunity to watch the best baseball players in the world gather together on one field, well that's something special to behold.

Now, the eats!

The obvious choices for food include beer, plus the prerequisite pizza and poppers. But why not treat yourself and your buddies to something homemade? Why not welcome them to the world of Bar Brawl Chili?

Bar Brawl Chili

Ingredients (for eight people, plus leftovers; you've gotta have leftovers!):

A couple of packages of chili powder
Three pounds of meat (burger meat is good)
One pound of Italian sausage
Salt
Garlic
Two big-ass onions
Jalapeño peppers
Fifty-plus ounces of canned tomatoes (minced, if you can)
Beer
Thirty-plus ounces of kidney beans
Thirty-plus ounces of black beans
Ten-plus ounces of baked beans
Can o' corn
Half-empty Tupperware containers full of whatever

What you do:

1. Crumble one or two pounds of meat into a frying pan and cook over medium heat till somewhere between rare and medium-rare. Dump fat into your empty beer can, put meat into a big pot. Cook the rest, repeating the whole process. Sprinkle some salt and the chili powder packets while browning.
2. Remove sausage meat from its natural casing and crumble or dice. Brown as above.
3. With 95 percent of the fat drained off, but a little left behind, brown diced onions, diced garlic, minced jalapeño peppers (number depends on how hot you like it, fella).
4. Dump this mixture into the pot with the browned meat.

5. Pour all of the canned tomatoes and corn into the pot, along with half a beer; a little more salt, too.

6. Have one more chili packet and one more can of minced tomatoes at the ready so that you can season to taste.

7. At this point, it's fun to check the fridge for leftovers. If it seems like it'd be decent—something like beef and Chinese vegetables, bacon bits, salsa, meatballs, roasted peppers, whatever—throw it in there!

8. Heat under the pot should be less than medium but more than a simmer. Stir every ten minutes. After twenty minutes or so, you should be ready to chow down. Know, though, that the second tasting will be better than the first. Reheating just brings out the juices. Or something culinary like that.

9. Don't forget to garnish with whatever you'd like (I dig cheese). Also, drink a couple of beers. Everything tastes better after a couple of beers.

Chili on the couch is one way I get my body back into softball shape.

The name Bar Brawl Chili has a meaning, but it's really the stuff of fabrication. You see, originally I called this recipe Kitchen Sink Chili because I'd throw in everything but the kitchen sink. But then I got this image in my head of somebody eating the chili, going out for some adult beverages, and then letting loose a fart at the bar. This fart smells so bad, as my imagination tells it, that somebody takes a swing at the guy. A bar brawl ensues . . . Fear not, though. This has never actually happened, so you can eat safely. Besides, you're not going anywhere, anyway. If you care about a ball game, I am of the opinion that it is best viewed at home.[29] I believe that like I believe chili is healthy. With all my heart!

---

[29] *Unless, of course, you have tickets to game 7 of an ALCS between the Yankees and Red Sox. Then, all bets are off!*

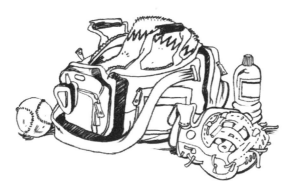

Closing: You're Never Too Old to Break Up a Double Play

George Carlin once asked, "Why do we sing 'Take Me Out to the Ballgame' when we're already there?"

Well, the answer is because we want to go back, because we want to be there again. And as players, we want to play again. Cracker Jack or no Cracker Jack.

But Carlin's quote is not without merit. It's important to be able to laugh about even those things we treasure. Baseball was once one of those things if you've made the switch like I have. But for some, softball has always been the passion. More and more girls are playing Little League baseball, but in turn, more and more towns are offering youth softball leagues for girls. They know it's on a softball field where, most likely, these girls will compete in high school and then, hopefully, in college.[30]

That being said, for many women softball has always been the love. They've always wanted to be taken out to those ball games. Guys, we're a little slow to pick up on the finer things in life: hand-rolled cigars, Mickey O'Rourke films, the fourth out-fielder! But once we're in, hook, line, and sinker, the appreciation blossoms. We lie to get out of meetings just to be there for the first pitch, we play through aches and pains just to get one more at-bat, we drop cash on equipment in hopes of regaining that lost step or swing, we throw ourselves, body and soul, into the game we now call our own.

There is nothing wrong with being a weekend warrior. Some might use the phrase in a critical way, but there's no need for a negative connotation. Why should games be just for kids? Who said that working, home ownership, and reproducing means an end to fun? If depression and obesity are ravaging the land, then let's fight back, I say. With all that we've got, let's send the Grim Reaper scurrying back to first with nothing but a long single. Let's strand him there and then take *our* cuts!

Now, let's say it's been about fifteen years since you last swung a bat. Your arms have deflated like balloons, your back is tighter than a tennis racquet, your vision is so bad that you now must wear rec specs, and because of all of the above you couldn't hit a key lime pie pitched underhand by Emeril, even if you had that tennis racquet in hand. Go down to the field, anyway.

---

[30] *That being said, a nod to Monique Ardissone. Not only did Big Mo lead my Little League (not just my team, the entire league!) in home runs, as a senior in high school she quit softball to take her shot with the varsity baseball team. You go, Mo!*

You can still toss the ball back in to the infield, can't you? In the least, you can crouch behind home plate to catch for an inning or two, right? I hope you've got dexterity enough to wave a guy home! There's always a need for base coaches.

So, my aging friend, quit making excuses. Lace up the old cleats. Dust off the old mitt and dig one of those stinky hats you used to wear out of the back of the closet. Play ball.

Softball is not an overly physical game. I don't come home sore unless I've done something stupid like slide head-first. And even then, sore is relative. A marshmallow is never sore, so that's why it hurts so much the first time. But the best part is—and hopefully you haven't forgotten this feeling—that you not only get used to the postgame soreness, you remember to relish it!

Even if you're no longer fast, you can apply your smarts and be a good base runner.

Matt contributes in ways big and small. In this case, he tells Joe to slide, slide, slide.

Even if you're no longer strong, you can poke an opposite-field hit to move the runner into scoring position.

Even if you feel out of touch with the lingo, you can yell, "SLIIIIDE!" as your man comes home, the throw zooming in like a heat-seeking missile.

Even if your throwing arm is shot, you can shot-put the ball back to the pitcher. You can keep the books. You can contribute.

And you know what, whether or not you really do anything, the guys on the other team will still say "Good game" as you shake hands. There is no clearer sign that you're back in the mix. For the first time in a long time, you've got opponents and you've got teammates. And without swelling the heads of my fellow Payne Environmentalists, that's the best part. Don't deny yourself the camaraderie, man. You're never too old to play the game. No matter how good you once were and how bad you are now, as Neil Young and Def Leppard remind us, it's better to strike out than fade away.

That's all from this weekend warrior. I can only spend so much time sitting in front of this computer. I need to play catch. I need to dive in the dirt. I need to take some batting practice. I need to banter with the fellas, whether it's at the ball field or the bar. I know that it's not just fun, that it's good for me. Body and soul. So, off I go. Ragged cleats, trusty glove, athletic supporter, used socks, and a hat that smells even worse. Smells so bad, but so good. So very, very good.

Bibliography

http://www.asasoftball.com/

*http://www.baseballlibrary.com/baseballlibrary/ballplayers/R/Rotisserie
_League_Baseball.stm*

Dickson, Paul. *The Worth Book of Softball.* New York: Facts on File, Inc. 1994.

Juba, Kelvin. *Swimming for Fitness.* Guilford, Connecticut: The Lyons Press. 2002.

http://www.kingandhiscourt.com/

Kleiner, Susan M. and Greenwood-Robinson, Maggie. *High-Performance Nutrition.* New York: John Wiley & Sons. 1996.

McCrory, G. Jacobs. *Softball Rules in Pictures.* New York: Perigee Books. 1987.

http://www.softballperformance.com/tips.shtml

http://softballsearch.eteamz.com/services.html

Vickery, Donald M. and Fries, James F. *Take Care of Yourself.* Reading, Massachusetts: Addison-Wesley Publishing Company, Inc. 1992.

Von Hoffman, Todd. *The Big Damn Book of Sheer Manliness.* Santa Monica, California: General Publishing Group, Inc. 1997.